Buckle Down!™

on Ohio Science

Second Edition

Buckle Down
PUBLISHING COMPANY

ACKNOWLEDGEMENT:

Buckle Down Publishing gratefully acknowledges the contributions of Rollin Bannow to the development of *Buckle Down on Ohio Science*. Mr. Bannow is a veteran science teacher with considerable experience in developing tests and curriculum materials. His writing projects include the science performance assessments for the *Iowa Tests of Basic Skills* and testing materials for the North Carolina Department of Public Instruction. Mr. Bannow has also served as science editor for other *Buckle Down* workbooks.

Buckle Down Publishing also gratefully acknowledges the valuable input of numerous Ohio science teachers in the design and revision of this program.

ISBN 0-7836-1540-X

Catalog #BD OH9S 1   4 5 6 7 8 9 10

Cover art: Images © 1996 PhotoDisc, Inc.

TABLE OF CONTENTS

Introduction

You've Been a Scientist Nearly All of Your Life

Science was one of your first activities. When you were just a little tot, you were curious about everything around you. In science, that's called **observation**. When you were old enough to say a few words, you said something like "doggie" every time you saw an animal. An older person probably started to correct you if what you saw was actually a cat. Scientists call this **classification**. To separate the big dogs from the small ones, you started to compare their size to something else. For example, the dog was either larger or smaller than your teddy bear. That's the beginning of **measuring**. Later you learned to compare sizes to standard measures like meters or grams.

When you heard that Spot, the mother dog, weighed a lot more than her pup Sparky, you began to see some relationships among observations. First you saw that organisms start small and get larger, which was true for you and your parents, too. You also learned to recognize the **pattern** that "smaller" often means lighter in weight. When you spotted a large and a small robin in the yard, you were able to **infer** something about their relative ages and weights. **Inferring** is a way of *processing* knowledge.

You then *extended* your knowledge by **predicting** that some day the two robins would be similar in size. However, you also at some point realized that your **hypotheses** were not always correct. A large sponge might be lighter than a smaller rock. You learned to constantly **evaluate** your ideas and **ask questions** that would lead you to more accurate **models** of how the world works.

One more thing: the word "No." When your parents thought that you were doing something that could hurt you, they'd say, "No!" Scientists call the no-no's **safety rules**. You should learn them and use them.

Throughout this book, you'll get a chance to continue to do science like you've always done it. Each unit has opportunities for you to **Act Like a Scientist** and to **Think Like a Scientist**. In addition, you'll get to practice showing other people that you really are a scientist by **Testing Like a Scientist** throughout the book. Finally, you'll have the opportunity to learn even more about how to take science tests when you **Become an Editor of Science Tests** at the end of each unit in the **Get the BEST of the Test** section.

The table below shows where the Ohio ninth-grade science outcomes are covered in this workbook.

State Outcome	Unit	Discovery Module	Test Like a Scientist Items
1. Devise a classification system for a set of objects or a group of organisms	1	1 2 3	2, 8 3 5, 6
2. Distinguish between observation and inference given a representation of a scientific situation	1	1 2 3	1, 4, 9, 10 1, 2, 5 1, 2
3. Identify and apply science safety procedures	4	11	1, 2, 3, 4
4. Demonstrate an understanding of the use of measuring devices and report data in appropriate units	1	1 2 3	3 4, 6 10
5. Describe the results of earth-changing processes	2	5	1, 2, 3, 4
6. Apply concepts of the earth's rotation, tilt, and revolution to an understanding of time and season	3	8	1, 2, 3, 4, 5, 6
7. Describe interactions of matter and energy throughout the lithosphere, hydrosphere, and atmosphere	2	5	6, 7, 8, 9
8. Apply the use of simple machines to practical situations	3	9	3, 4, 5, 6
9. Apply the concept of force and mass to predict the motion of objects	3	9	9, 10, 11, 12
10. Apply the concepts of energy transformations in electrical and mechanical systems	3	9	1, 2, 7, 8
11. Apply concepts of sound and light waves to everyday situations	2	6	1, 2, 3, 4, 5
12. Describe chemical and/or physical interactions of matter	1	3	3, 4, 7, 8, 9
13. Trace the flow of energy and/or interrelationships of organisms in an ecosystem	2	4	1, 2, 4, 5
14. Compare and contrast the characteristics of plants and animals	1	1	6, 11, 12
15. Explain biological diversity in terms of the transmission of genetic characteristics	3	7	1, 2, 3, 4, 5, 6
16. Describe how organisms accomplish basic life functions at various levels of organization and structure	1	1	5, 7
17. Describe the ways scientific ideas have changed using historical contexts	4	10	1, 2, 3, 4
18. Compare renewable and nonrenewable resources and strategies for managing them	2	4	8, 9, 10, 11
19. Describe the relationship between technology and science	4	10	5, 6, 7, 8
20. Describe how a given environmental change affects an ecosystem	2	4	3, 6, 7

UNIT ONE

Acquiring Scientific Knowledge

The Ohio State Department of Education expects you to demonstrate the ability to perform 20 basic science tasks. Unit 1 covers the following topics:

- Devise a classification system for a set of objects or a group of organisms. (Outcome 1)

- Distinguish between observation and inference given a representation of a scientific situation. (Outcome 2)

- Demonstrate an understanding of the use of measuring devices and report data in appropriate units. (Outcome 4)

- Describe chemical and/or physical interactions of matter. (Outcome 12)

- Compare and contrast the characteristics of plants and animals. (Outcome 14)

- Describe how organisms accomplish basic life functions at various levels of organization and structure. (Outcome 16)

Discovery Module 1: Life Science

Like little kids, scientists observe everything around them. Measurements are used to help scientists describe their observations. In this section you will sharpen your information-gathering skills.

Act Like a Scientist

Describe your thumb. Use at least one characteristic detected by each of your senses.

_____

_____

_____

_____

Think Like a Scientist

1. Which sense did you use to get most of the information about your thumb?

   _____

2. What inferences can you make about your thumb? That is, what logically follows from what you observed?

   _____

   _____

   _____

   _____

3. What measuring devices or instruments would help you describe your thumb in more detail, or in a more precise way?

   _____

   _____

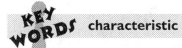
KEY WORDS   *characteristic*   *inference*

Test Like a Scientist

In the questions below, use your information-gathering skills to make observations.

Use the illustrations below to answer question 1.

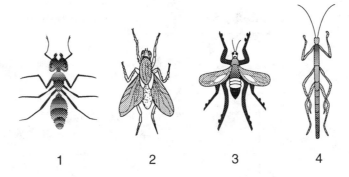

1   2   3   4

1. In what way are these organisms similar?
    A. length of antennae
    B. kind of mouth parts
    C. shape of wings
    D. number of legs

    Reasoning: State your reason or reasons for selecting the answer. (Include only directly observable characteristics.)

    _____

    _____

    _____

    _____

KEY WORDS observation

Use the following information to answer question 2.

Another way of describing something is to classify it. One kind of classification is based upon the arrangement of an object's or organism's parts. The manner in which the parts mirror each other determines its symmetry. Several types of symmetry are shown in the table.

Type of Symmetry	Example	Description
bilateral	←─ or ⋈	Two (*bi*) sides (*lateral*) that are the same.
radial	✳	Identical parts extending from a central point on an axis. Like spokes on a wheel.
pentagonal	✶	Five (*pent*) identical parts extending from a central point or axis—a special form of radial symmetry.

2. Which of these organisms does NOT exhibit bilateral symmetry?

A.

B.

C.

D.

Reasoning: State your reason or reasons for selecting the answer. (Explain the term "bilateral symmetry" in your reasoning.)

_____

_____

_____

_____

KEY WORDS symmetry   bilateral   radial   pentagonal

When measurements are used for describing, the choice of units is always important.

Use the following diagram to answer questions 3–6.

This plant has been growing in the water for three days.

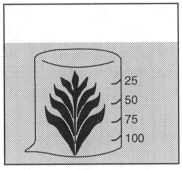

Start   After 3 Days

3. What unit is being used to measure the volume of gas in the experiment?
   A. centimeters
   B. milliliters
   C. millimeters
   D. centigrams

   Reasoning: State your reason or reasons for selecting the answer. (Use a form of the terms "mass," "length," and "capacity.")

   _____

   _____

   _____

Sometimes classification is based upon an object's or organism's source of energy.

4. What source of energy is required for the gas layer to form?
   A. sugar
   B. light
   C. water
   D. oxygen

   Reasoning: State your reason or reasons for selecting the answer. (Use a form of the word "photosynthesis.")

   _____

   _____

   _____

KEY WORDS   mass   length   capacity   gram   meter   liter   photosynthesis

Knowing the characteristics of two organisms or objects allows scientists to make assumptions about the interactions between them.

5. What substances provided by the plant allow animals to live in water?
    A. oxygen and food
    B. oxygen and water
    C. food and carbon dioxide
    D. carbon dioxide and water

    Reasoning: State your reason or reasons for selecting the answer. (Try to include the general chemical reactions for respiration and photosynthesis in your reasoning.)

    _____

    _____

    _____

Scientists use classification systems to make inferences about organisms' differences and similarities.

6. What accounts for the fact that animals carry out respiration at a higher rate than plants?
    A. Only plants use the sun's energy.
    B. Animals eat more food than plants.
    C. Only plants get energy from fermentation.
    D. Animals move around more than plants.

    Reasoning: State your reason or reasons for selecting the answer. (Use the key word "oxygen.")

    _____

    _____

    _____

KEY WORDS respiration   oxygen

Scientists often make careful observations to learn about the behavior of organisms and the operation of their parts.

Use the following pictures to answer question 7.

A scientist made the following diagrams to describe the operation of the human heart. You will acquire information by observing them.

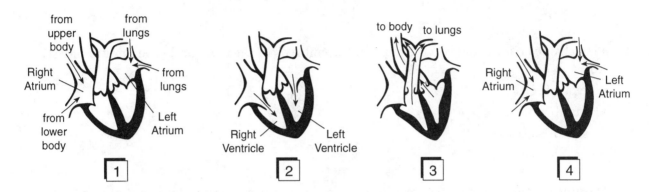

7. Which of the following best identifies the process shown in the sequence of pictures? (Note: "Atria" is the plural form of "atrium.")

A. Blood is circulated within the heart from the left to the right side.

B. Blood from the ventricles enters the atria, which pump it directly to the body.

C. Blood enters the heart through the atria and is pumped out through the ventricles.

D. Ventricles pump blood to the atria and then out of the heart to the rest of the body.

Reasoning: State your reason or reasons for selecting the answer. (Summarize the heart sequence shown, including the source and destination of the blood at each step.)

_____

_____

_____

_____

KEY WORDS   atrium   ventricle

Use the following information to answer question 8.

In a culture dish, the following stages of development were observed.

 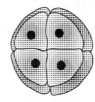 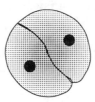

8. What characteristic could you use to put these embryos in chronological (youngest to oldest) order?

   A. type of cells
   B. number of cells
   C. size of embryo
   D. position of cells

   Reasoning: State your reason or reasons for selecting the answer. (Use a form of the word "mitosis.")

   _____

   _____

   _____

   _____

KEY WORDS   embryo   cell   mitosis

Use the picture to answer question 9.

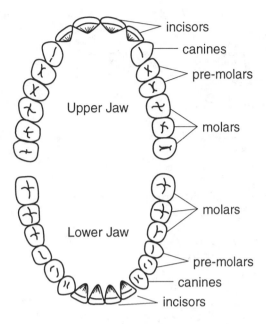

incisors

canines

pre-molars

Upper Jaw

molars

molars

Lower Jaw

pre-molars

canines

incisors

9. What is the advantage of having a variety of human teeth shapes?
    A. Each shape has a specialized chewing function.
    B. The different shapes allow all of the teeth to fit in our mouths.
    C. The incisors improve our appearance, while the molars chew.
    D. The variety helped human ancestors chew, but is not needed in modern humans.

    Reasoning: State your reason or reasons for selecting the answer. (Explain how each tooth shape helps accomplish its function. Use a form of the word "omnivore.")

    _____

    _____

    _____

    _____

KEY WORDS *omnivore*

Use the picture to answer question 10.

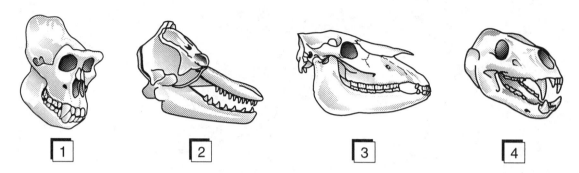

10. Which of these sets of teeth is adapted especially for herbivores?

   A. 1
   B. 2
   C. 3
   D. 4

Reasoning: State your reason or reasons for selecting the answer. (Define "herbivore" and explain how the set of teeth that you chose helps it to obtain and/or chew its food.)

_____

_____

_____

_____

© 1998 Profiles Corporation. DO NOT DUPLICATE.

Plant and animal characteristics are reflected at the cellular level.

Use the pictures of a plant cell and an animal cell to answer questions 11 and 12.

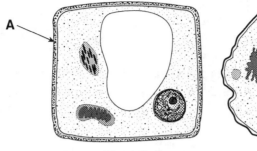

Plant Cell 　　　　　　　 Animal Cell

11. Why do plant cells, but not animal cells, contain structure A?

    A. to provide support for the plant

    B. to give off oxygen and carbon dioxide

    C. to enable the plant to absorb sunlight

    D. to prevent cells from uncontrolled growth

    Reasoning: State your reason or reasons for selecting the answer. (Use the term "cell wall.")

    _____

    _____

    _____

12. What characteristic requires that structure A be absent from animal cells?

    A. Animals move to obtain food.

    B. Animals have sexual reproduction.

    C. Animals contain many organ systems.

    D. Animals take in oxygen and give off carbon dioxide.

    Reasoning: State your reason or reasons for selecting the answer. (First describe structure A. Then explain how it relates to your answer choice.)

    _____

    _____

    _____

 **cell wall**

Discovery Module 2: Earth Science

Observing, measuring, and classifying are also important methods of learning about earth science.

Act Like a Scientist

Directions: Crumple a sheet of stiff paper or lightweight oak tag into a ball. Uncrumple it somewhat, but do not smooth it out; simply pull the edges and corners apart. You now have a model of a section of the earth's surface. The highest parts are the tops of mountains or hills. The lowest parts are the bottoms of rivers and lakes.

Imagine that it is spring and that snow is melting on the tops of the mountains. Using colored markers, pencils, or crayons, draw blue lines to show where you think streams and rivers would run. Use blue to color in sections where you think lakes would form. Use brown to show land that is too steep for many plants to grow on. Shade areas green to show where you think plants would grow. If time permits, use your creativity to show artificial structures, such as buildings or bridges.

Think Like a Scientist

1. In what ways is the paper like the earth's surface?

   _____

   _____

   _____

2. How did you choose the paths for your rivers and lakes?

   _____

   _____

   _____

3. In what way is crumpling the paper similar to changes that occur in the earth's surface over long periods of time?

   _____

   _____

   _____

Test Like a Scientist

Visual observations are important when placing an object into a classification system.

Use the following pictures of galaxies to answer questions 1 and 2.

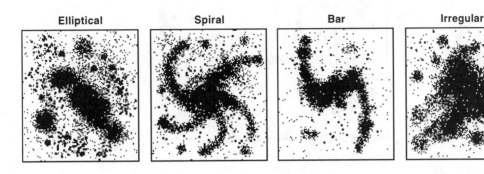

Galaxies are classified by their shapes as viewed from the earth.

1. Which type of galaxy is shown at the right?

   A. elliptical   C. bar

   B. spiral   D. irregular

   Reasoning: State your reason or reasons for selecting the answer. (Describe the type of galaxy you chose. Then describe ways in which the galaxy in the question is similar to the type of galaxy you selected.)

   _____

   _____

   _____

Visual observations can often be useful in making inferences about the origin and movement of an object or system.

2. Based upon the shapes of the spiral and bar galaxies, which statement about the movement of the individual stars within them is correct?

   A. The stars definitely are rotating.   C. The stars apparently are not rotating.

   B. The stars apparently are rotating.   D. The stars definitely are not moving.

   Reasoning: State your reason or reasons for selecting the answer. (Include the difference between an observation and an inference.)

   _____

   _____

   _____

Use the following information to answer question 3.

This is a map of the larger Hawaiian Islands:

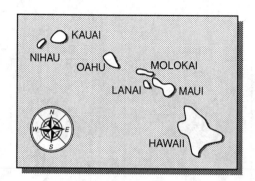

The Hawaiian Islands are all located on the same crustal plate of the earth. The oldest islands shown are at the top and left of the map. Each island in the chain is progressively younger, with the island of Hawaii being the youngest. The islands were made by volcanoes.

These volcanoes were formed over a single, stationary hot spot that exists beneath the plate on which they are located. Think of this portion of the earth's crust as a piece of paper that is being moved over a stationary candle flame. As the paper moves over the flame, scorch marks appear on the paper. These scorch marks represent volcanic islands.

3.   In what direction is this crustal plate moving?

   A.   NW

   B.   SE

   C.   SW

   D.   NE

Reasoning: State your reason or reasons for selecting the answer. (You might want to use the scorch-mark idea in your explanation.)

_____

_____

_____

_____

Scientists rely upon specific tools to measure particular characteristics.

Use the following information to answer question 4.

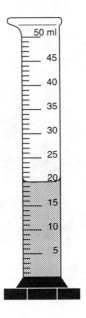 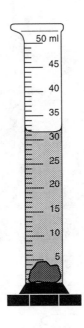

4. What property of the rock is being measured?

A. mass

B. solubility

C. length

D. volume

Reasoning: State your reason or reasons for selecting the answer. (Use the term "graduated cylinder.")

_____

_____

_____

_____

KEY WORDS graduated cylinder

Practice your powers of observation on the following diagram, then answer questions 5 and 6.

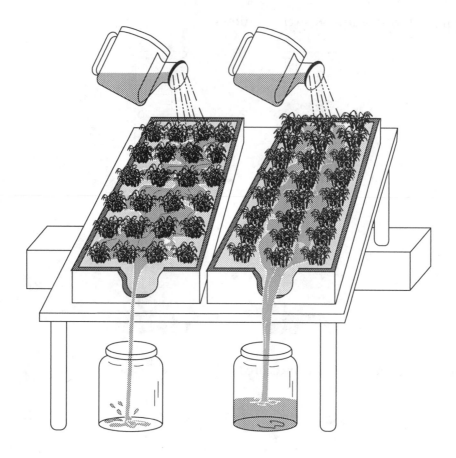

5. What is being compared in the demonstration?

    A. type of soil

    B. slope of soil

    C. covering over soil

    D. amount of water poured

Reasoning: State your reason or reasons for selecting the answer. (In your reasoning, describe a visible difference between the two trays.)

_____

_____

_____

_____

6. What unit of measure would be most appropriate for measuring the volume of water in the jars?

    A. milliliters
    B. kilograms
    C. decimeters
    D. centimeters

    Reasoning: State your reason or reasons for selecting the answer. (Use one of these key terms: "volume" or "capacity.")

    _____

    _____

    _____

    _____

KEY WORDS   volume   capacity

Discovery Module 3: Physical Science

Observing, measuring, and classifying are important ways of collecting information in physical science, too.

Act Like a Scientist

Directions: Obtain a container of lukewarm water.

Step 1: Dip your finger in the water. Note whether the water feels warmer, colder, or the same temperature as your finger. Circle the word in the table below that describes your observation.

Step 2: Pull your finger out of the water. Hold it still. Record the water temperature on your finger compared to that in step one. Circle the word that describes your observation.

Step 3: Wave your finger through the air. Record the water temperature relative to that in Step 2. Again, circle the word that describes your observation.

Step	Relative Temperature (circle higher, same, or lower)
1	higher same . . . than temperature of dry finger lower
2	higher same . . . than temperature of finger Step 1 lower
3	higher same . . . than temperature of finger Step 2 lower

Think Like a Scientist

1. What do you observe happening to the water on your finger as you hold it in the air?

   _____

   _____

   What can you infer about where the water is going?

   _____

   _____

   _____

2. What do you observe happening to the temperature of your finger as you hold it in the air?

   _____

   _____

   What can you infer is causing the change to occur?

   _____

   _____

   _____

3. What do you observe about both the rate of drying and the temperature of your finger as you wave it through the air?

   _____

   _____

   What inference can be made about your observations?

   _____

   _____

   _____

Characteristics used for classification are helpful for predicting interactions of matter.

Test Like a Scientist

Use the following information to answer questions 1 and 2.

Matter can exist in three states: solid, liquid, and gas. Solids have a definite volume and shape; liquids have a definite volume and varying shape; and gases have no definite shape or volume.

1. Ohio has underground deposits of natural gas, oil, and coal. Choose the table that shows their proper classification.

A.

solid	liquid	gas
coal	oil	natural gas

C.

solid	liquid	gas
oil	natural gas	coal

B.

solid	liquid	gas
natural gas	coal	oil

D.

solid	liquid	gas
coal	natural gas	oil

Reasoning: State your reason or reasons for selecting the answer. (Use the descriptions of each state of matter provided in the paragraph above.)

_____

_____

_____

2. Which type of substance can be sent from one part of the country to another through a pipeline?
   A. gas only
   B. liquid only
   C. gas and liquid
   D. solid and liquid

Reasoning: State your reason or reasons for selecting the answer. (Think about what characteristic would help a substance pass through a long, curved pipeline.)

_____

_____

_____

 solid   liquid   gas

Use the following information to answer questions 3 and 4.

There are two basic ways in which matter can be combined. One type of combination represents a physical change. In a physical change, substances change physical properties but not their chemical properties. They can be separated again by physical means.

The other type of combination represents a chemical change. A chemical change produces new substances with new chemical properties.

3. Which of the following combinations represents a chemical change?
   A. combining dirt and water to make mud
   B. mixing vinegar and baking soda to make bubbles
   C. adding water to sugar to make a sweet drink
   D. stirring salt and pepper to make a special seasoning

Reasoning: State your reason or reasons for selecting the answer. (In your reasoning, describe the new substance that was produced.)

_____

_____

_____

_____

In the snow belt along Lake Erie, the Ohio Department of Transportation sometimes spreads salt on the roads during the winter.

4. What change occurs to allow salt to slow the formation of ice on roads?
   A. a chemical change involving the salt and the road
   B. a chemical change involving the salt and water
   C. a physical change involving the salt and the road
   D. a physical change involving the salt and water

Reasoning: State your reason or reasons for selecting the answer. (Use a form of the term "freezing point.")

_____

_____

_____

_____

physical change   chemical change   freezing point

The five senses are important tools for making observations and for determining classification.

Use the following information to answer questions 5 and 6.

Another type of change is a phase change. For example, when water is warmed past its boiling point, it changes to a gas: water vapor. When it is cooled past its freezing point, it changes to a solid: ice. The phase changes can be described as follows:

Name of Change	Form of Change
evaporation	liquid to gas
condensation	gas to liquid
freezing	liquid to solid
melting	solid to liquid

5. Which observation is the direct result of evaporation?
   A. feeling wind on your skin
   B. hearing a sound from a trumpet
   C. smelling perfume across a room
   D. seeing raindrops on your shirt

   Reasoning: State your reason or reasons for selecting the answer. (In your explanation, identify the change of state that occurs.)

   _____

   _____

   _____

   _____

KEY WORDS   phase change   evaporation

6. Which situation represents condensation?

   A.

   C.

   B.

   D.

Reasoning: State your reason or reasons for selecting the answer. (Define "condensation" in your explanation.)

_____

_____

_____

_____

KEY WORDS condensation

Scientists acquire knowledge by carefully studying experimental data.

Use the following information to answer question 7.

A student heated a mixture of water and alcohol. Both liquids reached their boiling points during this procedure. The temperature of the mixture is given in the table.

Time (minutes)	1	2	3	4	5	6	7	8	9	10
Temp. (°C)	43	58	75	78	78	78	85	96	100	100

7. Which conclusion can be drawn from this experiment?
   A. Water and alcohol boil at 100°C.
   B. Alcohol and water boil at 78°C.
   C. Water boils at 100°C and alcohol boils at 43°C.
   D. Alcohol boils at 78°C and water boils at 100°C.

Reasoning: State your reason or reasons for selecting the answer. (Explain why the temperature of a boiling liquid is constant.)

_____

_____

_____

_____

KEY WORDS boiling point

By comparing experimental observations to verified findings, scientists can draw conclusions about the nature of a substance.

Use the following information to answer question 8.

The relative chemical activity of a piece of metal can be determined by placing it in a solution containing a different metal compound. If a reaction occurs, the piece of metal added is more reactive than the one in solution. If no reaction occurs, the metal in solution is more reactive than the piece of metal that was placed in it.

The following reactions were recorded in a lab.

Metal	Metal Compound	Reaction?
copper	lead nitrate	no
lead	iron (III) chloride	no
iron	copper nitrate	yes

8. Which conclusion fits the data?
   A. Copper is more reactive than lead.
   B. Copper is more reactive than iron.
   C. Lead is more reactive than iron.
   D. Iron is more reactive than copper.

Reasoning: State your reason or reasons for selecting the answer. (Explain what is most likely happening in the reaction represented by your choice.)

_____

_____

_____

_____

KEY WORDS compound

Use the following information to answer questions 9 and 10.

A student is trying to identify which of six unknown substances are metals. One of several tests for metals is to check for the production of hydrogen gas when the substance is placed in acid. The table below summarizes a series of chemical reactions from the student's experiments.

Substance	Water Reaction	Acid Reaction	Base Reaction
1	dissolves	dissolves	forms bubbles
2	insoluble	forms bubbles	insoluble
3	insoluble	insoluble	dissolves
4	insoluble	insoluble	insoluble
5	insoluble	forms bubbles	insoluble
6	dissolves	dissolves	forms bubbles

9. Based on the results so far, which substances should be tested further to confirm that they are metals?

    A. 1 and 6
    B. 2 and 5
    C. 3 and 4
    D. 5 and 6

Reasoning: State your reason or reasons for selecting the answer. (What inference can be made from the results that you chose?)

_____

_____

_____

_____

Acquiring useful information depends, in part, upon using appropriate tools.

10. One measure of water quality is its acidity. What measuring device would a scientist use to compare the acidity of the water in Ohio waters, such as Lake Loramie, Salt Fork Lake, and Caesar Creek?

   A. pH meter

   B. barometer

   C. thermometer

   D. graduated cylinder

   Reasoning: State your reason or reasons for selecting the answer. (Consider what each device measures.)

   _____

   _____

   _____

   _____

KEY WORDS pH

OHIO SCIENCE CONNECTIONS

Use the following information to answer questions 1-4.

Thomas Alva Edison was born in Milan, February 11, 1847, and spent his early childhood years in Ohio. When he was seven, his family moved to Michigan. Although young Thomas was not a successful student in school, he enjoyed reading science books and making models on his own. Edison took his first job at age 12 and proceeded to become a successful inventor and businessman without ever attending school again. Some things do change. Opportunities for 12-year-olds are very limited these days.

Several of the 1,093 United States patents awarded to Edison were related to his development of electric lights. While Edison was not the first to invent the incandescent light bulb, he and his laboratory staff performed many important experiments in an attempt to create a practical, long-lasting light bulb. One of their major challenges was to make the filament (the part that heats up and glows when electricity is passed through it) glow for more than a few seconds. One of Edison's solutions was to use carbon thread in a bulb from which most of the air had been removed.

Filament

1. What was gained by removing the air from the bulb?

    _____

    _____

    _____

    _____

2. The use of a carbon filament suggests that carbon has what property?

    A. It consumes air.   C. It glows without heating.

    B. It conducts electricity.   D. It burns in a vacuum.

    Reasoning: State your reason or reasons for selecting the answer. (Consider what purpose a filament serves in a light bulb.)

    _____

    _____

    _____

Edison also greatly improved the telephone transmitter, the part that changes your voice into an electrical signal. The principle of his carbon transmitter is shown below. The strength of the electric current is varied by the sound waves striking the diaphragm.

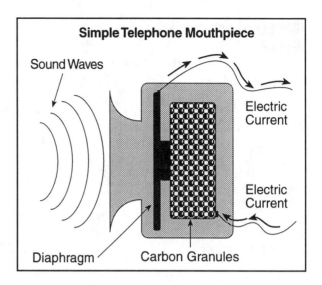

Simple Telephone Mouthpiece

Sound Waves

Electric Current

Electric Current

Diaphragm   Carbon Granules

3. When sound waves hit the carbon granules, the amount of electricity flowing through the carbon varies. What do the sound waves do to the carbon granules to cause these variations?

    A. magnetize them

    B. cause them to produce sound

    C. pack them tightly together

    D. make them produce electricity

    Reasoning: State your reason or reasons for selecting the answer. (Think about the action shown in the diagram.)

    _____

    _____

    _____

    _____

4. What property of sound does the operation of the transmitter suggest?

    A. Sound conducts electricity.

    B. Sound produces magnetism.

    C. Sound travels through electrical wires.

    D. Sound contains energy.

    Reasoning: State your reason or reasons for selecting the answer. (Once again, think about the action shown in the diagram.)

    _____

    _____

    _____

    _____

One More Thing

In this unit, you learned some characteristics of scientific investigation. You had a chance to act, think, and test like a scientist. To be a better test taker, you should also think a bit about tests themselves.

One of the best ways of learning is by doing. That's why at the end of each unit in this book you'll be asked to complete some activities that will help you to . . .

Get the BEST of the Test

 The way you'll do this is by practicing the skills needed to Become an Editor of Science Tests. You'll accomplish this by writing your own test questions and answers. Begin with the activities that follow.

Think about what you have learned in this unit. As you complete this section, keep in mind the important role of each of the following ways of acquiring scientific knowledge:

- observing,

- measuring, and

- classifying.

Use these pictures of seeds to complete questions 1–3.

   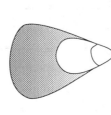      

1   2   3   4

1. Write an observation question about the seed types shown above.

_____

_____

2. Write an inference question about the seed types shown above.

_____

_____

3. Write a measurement question about the seed types shown on the previous page.

_____

_____

Use these pictures to answer question 4.

Complete the multiple-choice test item about these animals by creating the missing answer choices.

4. In what way are these animals similar?

Hint: Start with a correct answer; for example, they all have wings. Then find some other characteristics that are not shared by all three.

A. _____

B. _____

C. _____

D. _____

Use this situation to write a multiple-choice item about the change that has occurred over time:

5. _____

_____

_____

A. _____

B. _____

C. _____

D. _____

Proficiency Practice

Directions: Read each question and answer choice carefully. Circle the letter of the correct answer. Be prepared to discuss your answers in class.

Use the following information to answer question 1.

The parts of an object or organism can have many different arrangements. The manner in which the parts mirror each other determines its symmetry. Several types of symmetry are shown in the table.

Type of Symmetry	Example
bilateral	← or ⋈
radial	✳
pentagonal (special case of radial)	✴

1. Which of the following organisms has pentagonal symmetry?

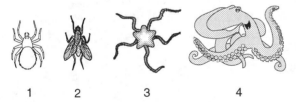

1 2 3 4

   A. 1
   B. 2
   C. 3
   D. 4

Use the following drawings of fossils to answer question 2.

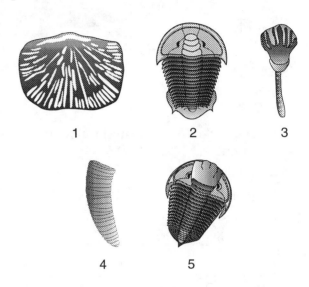

1 2 3

4 5

2. Judging by body structure, which two fossils are most closely related?

   A. 1 and 2
   B. 2 and 5
   C. 3 and 4
   D. 4 and 5

Use the following pictures to answer question 3.

3. What do all of these organisms have in common?

    A. pairs of wings

    B. length of tails

    C. number of legs

    D. sets of antennae

4. Which of the following combinations represents a physical change?

    A. baking a cake

    B. burning paper

    C. crushing rocks

    D. making concrete

Use the following information to answer question 5.

Birds' feet have adapted to their functions through the development of various structures.

5. Based only upon the foot's structure, what can you infer about this bird?

    A. It is able to fly swiftly.

    B. Its diet consists of fish.

    C. It migrates for the winter.

    D. It is adapted for swimming.

Use the following information to answer question 6.

Fish scales can be used to determine the age of a fish in the same way that tree rings can be used to measure the age of a tree.

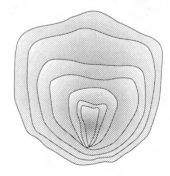

6. What is the age of the fish from which this scale was taken?

    A. 1 year

    B. 4 years

    C. 7 years

    D. 11 years

7. In which units would your doctor most
    likely measure a blood sample?

    A. kilograms

    B. milliliters

    C. milligrams

    D. centimeters

8. Which units would be most appropriate to
    measure the mass of medicine in a pill?

    A. milligrams

    B. centimeters

    C. milliliters

    D. kiloliters

9. In which units would the height of a
    volcano be measured?

    A. grams

    B. liters

    C. meters

    D. newtons

**Use the following information to answer
question 10.**

A spring that is stretched and released will
oscillate (bounce up and down). The greater the
weight on the end of the spring, the slower the
spring will oscillate.

The following weights are suspended, one at a
time, from the spring shown.

W = 30 g	X = 2 g
Y = 50 g	Z = 40 g

10. In what order can the weights be suspended
    so that the spring will oscillate faster on
    each trial?

    A. W, X, Y, Z

    B. X, W, Z, Y

    C. Z, Y, X, W

    D. Y, Z, W, X

Use the following information to answer question 11.

The graph shows how mercury's density changes with temperature.

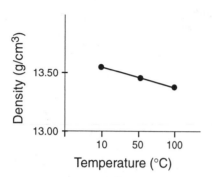

11. Which conclusion can be reached from this graph?
    A. Mercury expands as it is heated.
    B. Mercury shrinks as it is heated.
    C. Mercury neither shrinks nor expands upon heating.
    D. The data do not suggest shrinking or expanding.

12. The blocks of wood shown below are floating on water. What property would allow them to be ordered by percentage floating above the water?

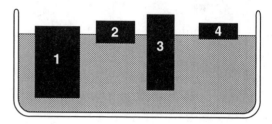

    A. mass
    B. weight
    C. size
    D. density

13. Which of the following is a valid statement to make when comparing plants to animals?
    A. Only plants can move.
    B. Only plants can make food.
    C. Only animals need water.
    D. Only animals require oxygen.

Use the following pictures to answer questions 14 and 15.

1

2

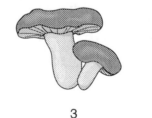

3

4

14. Which organism(s) carry(ies) out the process of photosynthesis?
    A. 2
    B. 3
    C. 2 and 3
    D. all of them

15. Which organisms carry out the process of respiration?
    A. 1 and 4
    B. 1 and 3
    C. 1, 3, and 4
    D. 1, 2, 3, and 4

Use the following to answer question 16.

This is a diagram of a sperm fertilizing an egg. The rods inside each represent chromosomes.

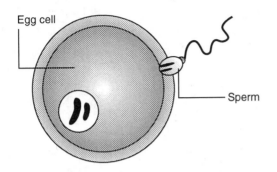

Egg cell

Sperm

16. How will the number of chromosomes in the zygote (organism formed by the fertilization) compare with the number in either the sperm or the egg?

    A. half

    B. double

    C. same

    D. quadruple

Use the following diagram to answer question 17.

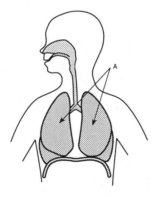

A

17. With what other organ does organ A cooperate most closely to carry out its function?

    A. heart

    B. liver

    C. brain

    D. stomach

Use the following diagram to answer question 18.

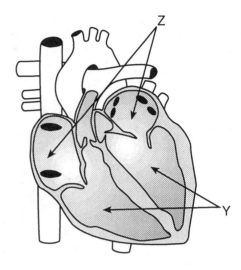

Z

Y

18. Which statement best compares the functions of chambers Y and Z?

    A. One pair pumps blood to the lungs, the other to the body.

    B. One pair is part of the heart, the other is part of the lungs.

    C. One pair receives blood, the other pumps it out of the heart.

    D. One pair handles oxygenated blood, the other deoxygenated blood.

UNIT TWO

Processing Scientific Knowledge

The Ohio State Department of Education expects you to demonstrate the ability to perform 20 basic science tasks. Unit 2 reviews the following topics:

- Describe the results of earth-changing processes. (Outcome 5)

- Describe interactions of matter and energy throughout the lithosphere, hydrosphere, and atmosphere. (Outcome 7)

- Apply concepts of sound and light waves to everyday situations. (Outcome 11)

- Trace the flow of energy and/or interrelationships of organisms in an ecosystem. (Outcome 13)

- Compare renewable and nonrenewable resources and strategies for managing them. (Outcome 18)

- Describe how a given environmental change affects an ecosystem. (Outcome 20)

Discovery Module 4: Life Science

If your parents have given you the pleasure of doing laundry (Hey, washing smelly gym socks is still better than being grounded), you are probably familiar with how clothes look after they come out of the drier. They're often wrinkled and crumpled. They need to be straightened, ironed, folded, or hung on hangers.

The data that scientists collect are something like clean, but rumpled, clothes. They need to be processed so that scientists can draw conclusions from them. One of your tasks in this unit is to process information.

Act Like a Scientist

Directions: Pretend that you've recently eaten a pizza topped with pepperoni and mushrooms. The primary ingredients are listed below. Complete the table by listing the main source of each ingredient. The first one has been completed for you.

Ingredient	Main Source
crust	grain
sauce	
cheese	
pepperoni	
mushroom	

In the space below, make a food web that includes yourself and the main food sources shown in the table.

KEY WORDS food web

Think Like a Scientist

1. What does a food web show?

   _____

   _____

   _____

   _____

2. How are food webs useful to scientists?

   _____

   _____

   _____

   _____

3. Why is it important for people to realize that they are part of food webs?

   _____

   _____

   _____

   _____

The ability to read and interpret visual displays of information (such as diagrams, tables, and graphs) is an important skill required for processing scientific information.

Test Like a Scientist

Use the following graph to answer questions 1–3.

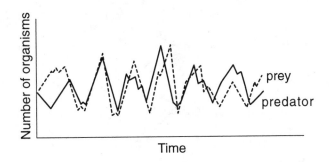

1. What does this graph show about the predator and prey populations?
    A. They remain stable over time.
    B. They are directly related.
    C. They show no relationship.
    D. They appear to be related.

    Reasoning: State your reason or reasons for selecting the answer. (Describe and explain the pattern that you observed.)

    _____

    _____

    _____

    _____

KEY WORDS   predator   prey

2. The relationship shown by the graph is most likely the result of which factor?
   A. food supplies
   B. disease epidemics
   C. hunting pressure
   D. habitat destruction

   Reasoning: State your reason or reasons for selecting the answer. (Explain how a predator's population is regulated by that of its prey, and vice versa.)

   _____

   _____

   _____

   _____

3. Which graph would likely represent the pattern that would occur if the food eaten by the prey became scarce?

   A.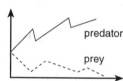

   C.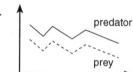

   B.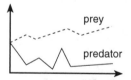

   D.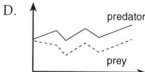

   Reasoning: State your reason or reasons for selecting the answer. (Explain how each population is affected in this situation.)

   _____

   _____

   _____

   _____

Use the following picture to answer questions 4–7

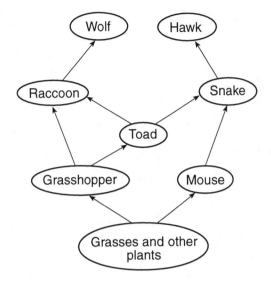

4. Which of the following describes the relationship between the raccoon and toad?

   A. predator-prey

   B. consumer-producer

   C. symbiotic partners

   D. parasite-host

Hint: What do the arrows signify?

Reasoning: State your reason or reasons for selecting the answer. (Explain each of the terms in your answer choice. Use the term "food web" or "food chain" in your answer.)

_____

_____

_____

_____

KEY WORDS   consumer   producer   parasite   host   symbiotic partners   food chain

Sometimes scientists must make inferences based upon the information they have.

5. What is the original source of energy for the hawk?
   A. snake
   B. mouse
   C. plants
   D. sun

   Reasoning: State your reason or reasons for selecting the answer. (Describe the energy sources by working backward from the hawk on the food web.)

   _____

   _____

   _____

   _____

Knowing the characteristics of an object or organism can help scientists to make predictions and evaluations.

6. If a rabbit were added to this web, with which organism(s) would it compete?
   A. plants
   B. mouse
   C. snake
   D. hawk

   Reasoning: State your reason or reasons for selecting the answer. (What do competitors have in common?)

   _____

   _____

   _____

   _____

7. An increase in the number of snakes would most likely result in which of the following changes?
   A. more mice
   B. fewer wolves
   C. fewer toads
   D. more raccoons

   Reasoning: State your reason or reasons for selecting the answer. (Discuss both the effect on what snakes eat and what eats snakes.)

   _____

   _____

   _____

   _____

8. Some automobiles are designed to run on alcohol, which can be produced from plant materials, such as corn. In what way would using plants as a source of energy be better than using oil made from petroleum?
   A. Plants are a renewable resource.
   B. Oil is a flammable safety hazard.
   C. Plants can be grown without cost.
   D. Oil is obtained only in foreign countries.

   Reasoning: State your reason or reasons for selecting the answer. (What is the long-range possibility in each case?)

   _____

   _____

   _____

   _____

KEY WORDS renewable resource

9. Ohio's coal and oil are formed from the remains of living organisms. Why are coal and oil considered nonrenewable resources?

A. Organisms that can form them no longer exist.

B. Their formation occurred only in the past.

C. There aren't as many organisms on earth today.

D. Their formation is too slow to cover present needs.

Reasoning: State your reason or reasons for selecting the answer. (Use a form of the terms "renewable" and "nonrenewable" in your explanation.)

_____

_____

_____

_____

10. Ohioans should consider which of the following as the most energy-efficient means of conserving nonrenewable resources?

A. Use only the ones in plentiful supply.

B. Reduce the use of these resources.

C. Recycle resources after they are used.

D. Use resources which are non-polluting.

Reasoning: State your reason or reasons for selecting the answer. (Define the term "energy efficient" in your explanation.)

_____

_____

_____

_____

KEY WORDS   nonrenewable resource   energy-efficient

11. Soil is a resource that is renewed as rocks break down and decayed organic material accumulates. Soil conservation is NOT accomplished by which of the following?

    A. crop rotation

    B. contour planting

    C. frequent plowing

    D. planting windbreaks

    Reasoning: State your reason or reasons for selecting the answer. (Use a form of the term "conservation" in your explanation.)

    _____

    _____

    _____

    _____

KEY WORDS conservation

Discovery Module 5: Earth Science

Act Like a Scientist

Situation: The earth's crust is made up of large plates, like the panels on a soccer ball. The plates are constantly moving: bumping into each other, sliding past each other, and going over and under each other. Plate boundaries are named for the type of motion taking place there.

Boundary Type	Movement of Plates	Diagram
convergent	toward each other	→ ←
divergent	away from each other	← — →
lateral	alongside each other	→ / ←

Directions: Use two 6-inch squares (approximate size) of cardboard or heavy paper to represent crustal plates. Move them around on your desk in the three types of motion shown in the table. Describe the results.

_____

_____

_____

_____

Think Like a Scientist

1. What kind of landform(s) might result from two converging plates?

   _____

   Give one example of this feature that exists on Earth today. (Hint: The crustal plate that holds India is converging with Asia.)

   _____

2. What might occur as two plates scrape past each other?

   _____

   Give one example of the result of this plate activity. (Hint: Parts of California are sliding against each other.)

   _____

3. What replaces plates that are spreading apart?

   _____

   Give one example of this geological feature. (Hint: Europe and Africa are pulling away from North and South America.)

   _____

Test Like a Scientist

Visual displays are useful for representing changes in the earth's crust that take place over time.

Use the following diagram to answer questions 1 and 2.

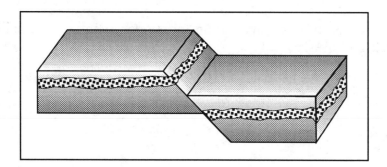

1. Which of the following forces would likely create the type of landform shown?
   A. pulling apart
   B. pushing together
   C. sliding sideways
   D. twisting around

   Reasoning: State your reason or reasons for selecting the answer. (Use a form of one of the following terms: "convergent," "divergent," or "lateral.")

   _____

   _____

   _____

   _____

2. Which of the following earth cross sections is most likely the site of a convergent fault?

A.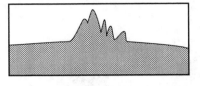

C.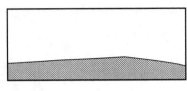

B.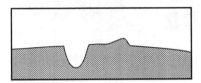

D.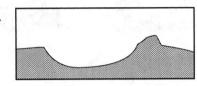

Reasoning: State your reason or reasons for selecting the answer. (Define the term "convergent fault" in your explanation.)

_____

_____

_____

_____

KEY WORDS   fault   convergent fault

3. Erosion changes mountains over time. What property of these profiles of different mountains can be used to order them by age?

A. height of peaks

B. width of bases

C. number of peaks

D. shape of peaks

Reasoning: State your reason or reasons for selecting the answer. (Define the terms "erosion" and "deposition" in your explanation.

_____

_____

_____

_____

Use the following diagram to answer question 4.

Rock Strata

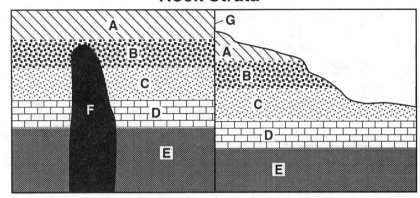

4. Which of the following sequences occurred in this formation?

   A. Fault G occurred before rock layer A was deposited.

   B. Rock layer D was deposited before intrusion F occurred.

   C. Rock layer C was deposited after rock layer B.

   D. Fault G occurred before rock layer E was deposited.

   Reasoning: State your reason or reasons for selecting the answer. (Complete a sequence of events for A, B, C, D, E, F, and G in your explanation.)

   _____

   _____

   _____

   _____

   _____

KEY WORDS intrusion

Use the contour map to answer question 5.

This is a contour map. Lines connect points of equal elevation.

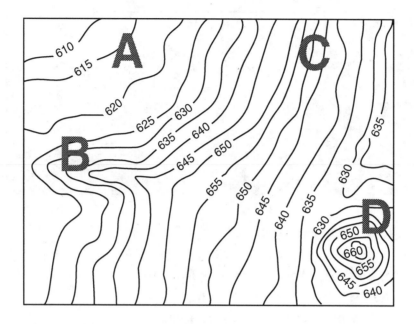

5. Which area could be farmed with the least chance of erosion?

    A. A

    B. B

    C. C

    D. D

    Reasoning: State your reason or reasons for selecting the answer. (Describe the surface features in each area.)

    _____

    _____

    _____

    _____

    _____

Use the following diagram to answer questions 6 and 7.

6. This diagram of the water cycle illustrates which of the following about water on earth?
    A. It is indestructible.
    B. It is becoming polluted.
    C. It is naturally recycled.
    D. Its volume is increasing.

    Reasoning: State your reason or reasons for selecting the answer. (Use a form of the terms "evaporate" and "condense.")

    _____

    _____

    _____

    _____

KEY WORDS   evaporate   condense

Diagrams can help scientists make inferences and predictions about the situations they illustrate.

7. The water cycle helps to explain which of the following?
    A. Chemicals that affect water vapor can affect surface water.
    B. Pollution in the ocean can affect the rain in Ohio.
    C. Chemical contamination of streams in Ohio can cause acid rain.
    D. Ocean water quality is not affected by surface water pollution.

    Reasoning: State your reason or reasons for selecting the answer. (Describe how the parts of your answer choice are linked.)

    _____

    _____

    _____

    _____

Use the following diagram to answer question 8.

Weather Map of the Continental United States

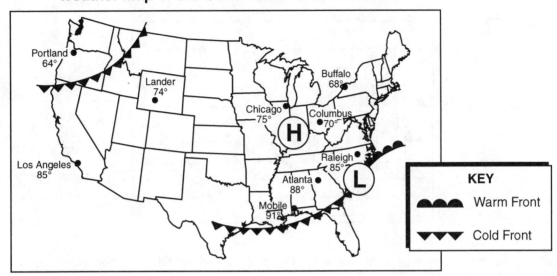

8. During the day shown above, the sky conditions in Columbus would produce which of the following?

A. no shadows

B. fuzzy shadows

C. low contrast shadows

D. high contrast shadows

Reasoning: State your reason or reasons for selecting the answer. (First, describe the Columbus sky conditions. Then decide which type of shadow would be produced under those conditions.)

_____

_____

_____

_____

Interpreting visual displays often requires an understanding of basic science concepts.

Use the following diagram to answer question 9.

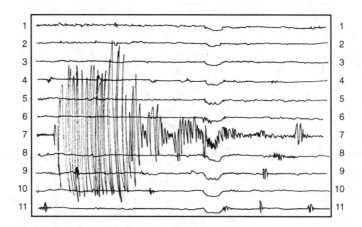

9. Look carefully at the type of motion recorded in line 7 above. In which of the following would such movement most likely occur?

   A. hydrosphere – all the water on the earth's surface

   B. lithosphere – the solid outer layer of the earth

   C. troposphere – the layer of the earth's atmosphere that contains water vapor

   D. stratosphere – the layer of gases between the troposphere and mesophere

   Reasoning: State your reason or reasons for selecting the answer. (First, describe the pattern of movements. Then explain the characteristic of your answer choice that would produce that pattern.)

   _____

   _____

   _____

   _____

 hydrosphere   lithosphere   troposphere   stratosphere   mesosphere

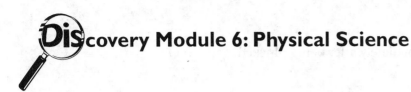

Discovery Module 6: Physical Science

Act Like a Scientist

Directions: Obtain a piece of heavy string or twine, approximately 150 cm long. Tie one end to a chair or table leg. While holding the other end, pluck it like a guitar string. Notice the tone. Then explore the following variables:

Length

Hold the string at about 2/3 its original length. Pluck it again. Record the sound difference in the table below.

Repeat the procedure with the string at about 1/3 its original length.

Tension

Hold the full length of the string loosely, but still tight enough to pluck. Pluck it and record the difference between that sound and the original sound.

Now hold it more tightly than the first time, pluck and record.

Transmitting Medium

Repeat one of the above procedures, but this time press the free end of the string between a finger and your cheek bone just in front of your ear. Record the difference.

Sound Variations

Variable	Difference between original sound and sound produced by variable
2/3 original length	
1/3 original length	
looser than original	
tighter than original	
string held to cheekbone	

Think Like a Scientist

1. What happened to the string immediately after being plucked?

   _____

   What was the immediate effect on the air surrounding the string?

   _____

2. When the string was shortened, what happened to its rate of vibration?

   _____

   _____

   _____

3. How did the vibration change as the tension on the string was increased?

   _____

   _____

   _____

4. Which appears to transmit sound more effectively, air or a solid such as bone?

   _____

   Explain your answer.

   _____

   _____

Test Like a Scientist

Visual displays of information also help scientists to understand physical science concepts.

Use the following information to answer question 1.

Sound can be represented by waves. The amplitude (height) of a wave describes its loudness, and the frequency (number of waves per unit of time) describes its pitch.

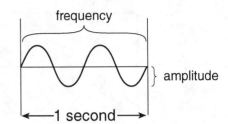

1. Which set of waves is in order from loudest to softest?

A.

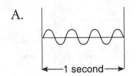 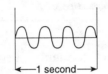

B.

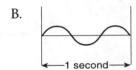 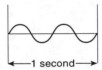 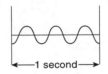

C.

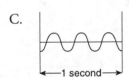 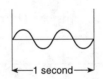

D.

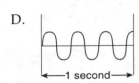 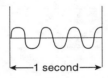 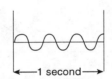

Reasoning: State your reason or reasons for selecting the answer. (Explain what variables you used to make your choice.)

_____

_____

_____

_____

KEY WORDS   frequency   amplitude

Use the following information to answer question 2.

The colors of a spectrum (rainbow) are determined by their wavelength. The following table provides a representative wavelength for the range covered by each color.

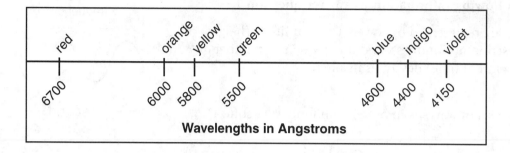

Wavelengths in Angstroms

2. A color, X, has a wavelength of 5,700 angstroms. Which sequence of colors progresses from shortest to longest wavelength?

   A. red, yellow, X, green

   B. orange, X, green, blue

   C. violet, blue, X, orange

   D. X, green, yellow, orange

   Reasoning: State your reason or reasons for selecting the answer. (List the actual wavelengths.)

   _____

   _____

   _____

   _____

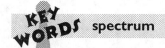 **spectrum**

Use the following lenses to answer question 3.

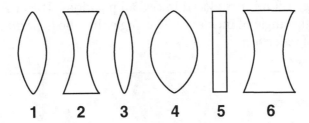

1   2   3   4   5   6

3. Which of the above lenses will cause light rays to converge (come together)?

 A. 1, 3, and 4

 B. 2, 5, and 6

 C. 3, 4, and 5

 D. 4, 6, and 1

 Reasoning: State your reason or reasons for selecting the answer. (Draw the paths of several light rays through the lenses of your choice. Consider what causes light to bend when it enters or leaves glass at an angle.)

_____

_____

_____

_____

Use the following information to answer question 4.

A flashlight beam is reflected off mirrors placed in several positions. The angle at which the beam strikes the mirror is called the angle of incidence. The angle that the departing beam forms with the mirror is called the angle of reflection.

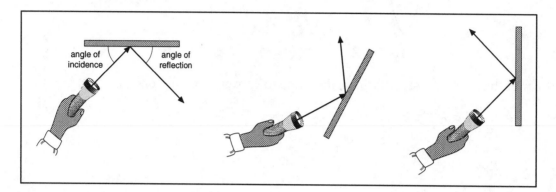

4. Which statement best identifies the property of reflection shown in the diagrams?

    A. The angles of incidence and reflection are of equal size.

    B. The sum of the angles of incidence and reflection is 180°.

    C. The sizes of the angles of incidence and reflection depend on the mirror angle.

    D. There is no relationship between the angles of incidence and reflection.

    Reasoning: State your reason or reasons for selecting the answer. (Explain what measurements you could make to prove your answer choice.)

    _____

    _____

    _____

    _____

Use the following information to answer question 5.

The speed of sound in water depends on the water's temperature. This is shown in the following graph.

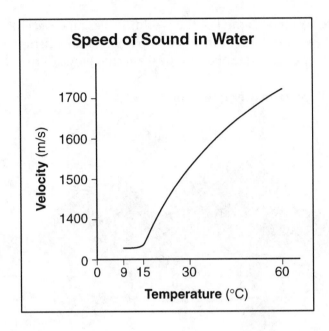

5. Which of the following is the best estimate of the speed of sound in water that is 40°C?

    A. 1500 m/s

    B. 1550 m/s

    C. 1600 m/s

    D. 1650 m/s

    Reasoning: State your reason or reasons for selecting the answer. (Draw on the graph as part of your explanation.)

    _____

    _____

    _____

    _____

OHIO SCIENCE CONNECTIONS

Lake Erie is known as the "Walleye Capital of the World." It has an especially rich supply of this variety of perch. In fact, several million of them end up hooked on a fishing line each year. Perch are fast-growing fish that are especially abundant in the western regions of the lake.

Use this picture of a walleye to answer questions 1 and 2.

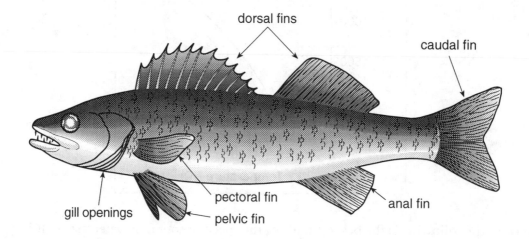

1. What are the pelvic fins most likely used for?
   A. capturing prey
   B. balance and turning
   C. high speed swimming
   D. a warning to predators

2. What feature is the best indicator that the walleye is a predator?
   A. sharp teeth in a large mouth
   B. large eyes on the sides of the head
   C. camouflage body markings on its side
   D. gill openings in front of its pectoral fins

The fish population in Lake Erie is affected by pollution levels in the lake. Lake Erie has a well-documented history of problems with pollution. In fact, in the 1960s, Lake Erie was labeled by some as a "dead lake." That label wasn't accurate, but did reflect serious pollution problems.

Use the profiles of the Great Lakes below to answer questions 3 and 4.

Profiles of the Great Lakes System

3. What feature suggests that Lake Erie is especially susceptible to accumulating high concentrations of pollutants?
   A. Lake Ontario is next to Lake Erie.
   B. The bottom of Lake Erie is not smooth.
   C. Lake Erie is almost level with other lakes.
   D. Lake Erie is the shallowest of the Great Lakes.

4. What would you compare to determine the direction of water flow from lake to lake through the Great Lakes?
   A. their deepest points
   B. their surface elevations
   C. their surface areas
   D. their total volume of water

Get the BEST of the Test

Remember, good test-makers make good test-takers. Your goal is to be a good test-taker, so let's practice a little test-making.

Use the skills you've developed in this unit to complete the following writing and editing activities.

Pretend that you have grown two identical rapid-growth plants in two different kinds of soil. You have cared for them in exactly the same way. The results are shown in the pictures below.

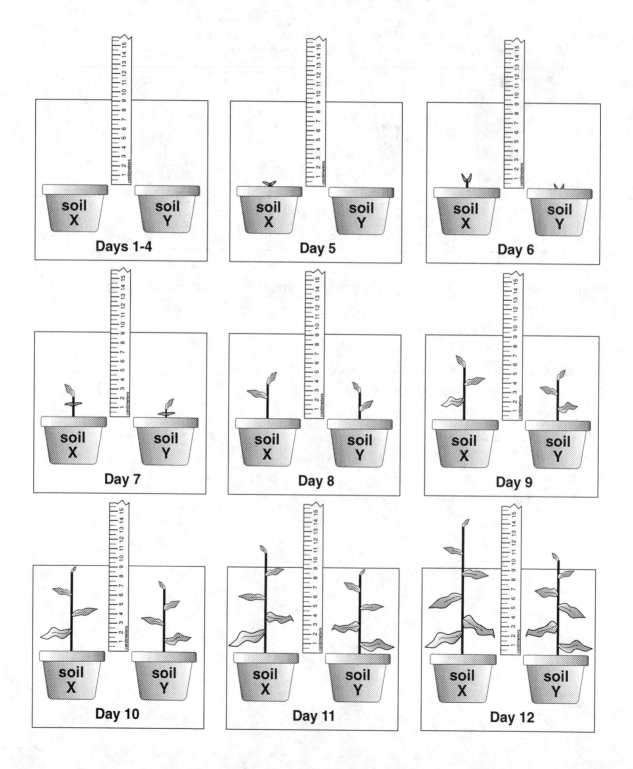

1. Make a table of the data. (Measure the height of the plant at the highest point.)

Days after planting	Height of plant (cm) Soil X	Height of plant (cm) Soil Y
1		
2		
3		
4		
5		
6		
7		
8		
9		
10		
11		
12		

2. Make a graph of the data in the table:

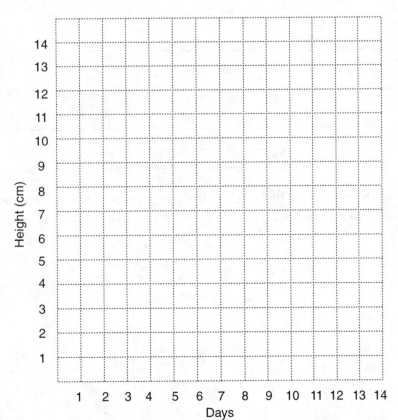

Write four questions that could be asked about this experiment.

3. _____

_____

4. _____

_____

5. _____

_____

6. _____

_____

Provide some possible answers for this question:

7. What would be the most likely height (in cm) of the plant grown in soil Y after one more day of growth?

A. _____

B. _____

C. _____

D. _____

Hint: The answer choices should be based on the pattern shown in the data, have a consistent difference between them, and not include any impossible heights.

Write a multiple-choice item dealing with a conclusion that could be drawn from this experiment.

8. _____

_____

_____

_____

_____

_____

_____

_____

_____

Proficiency Practice

Directions: Read each question and answer choice carefully. Circle the letter of the correct answer. Be prepared to discuss your answers in class.

Use the following information to answer question 1.

According to the theory of plate tectonics, the earth's crust is made up of large plates, like a soccer ball's panels. The boundaries between the plates are named as follows:

Boundary Type	Movement of Plates
convergent	toward each other
divergent	away from each other
lateral	alongside each other
static	no relative movement

The arrows show the movement of the upper mantle materials in the diagram below.

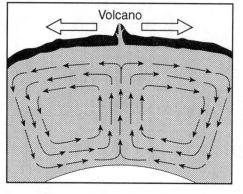

1. The volcano shown in the diagram resulted from what type of fault?
   A. static
   B. divergent
   C. lateral
   D. convergent

Use the following information to answer questions 2 and 3.

The data show age and polarity of sea-floor rock at various distances from the mid-Atlantic ridge. Polarity refers to the orientation of the magnetic minerals embedded in the rock.

Changes in the Atlantic Ocean Floor Over Millions of Years

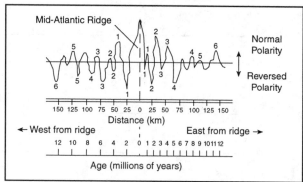

2. Based upon the data, which of the following changes seems most likely to happen at fairly regular intervals?
   A. The Atlantic Ocean depth changes.
   B. The Atlantic floor expands and contracts.
   C. The magnetic field of the earth reverses.
   D. The rocks on the Atlantic floor reverse direction.

3. Which science idea is supported by the data?
   A. plate tectonics
   B. expanding universe
   C. law of magnetic poles
   D. conservation of mass

4. What is the source of energy for the water cycle?

    A. oceans

    B. gravity

    C. clouds

    D. sun

Use the following picture to answer question 5.

5. To illustrate a part of the carbon cycle, arrows showing the direction of the carbon path could be drawn to which three objects?

    A. sun to deer to grass

    B. grass to fire to deer

    C. fire to grass to deer

    D. deer to grass to sun

Use the following diagram to answer question 6.

The core regions contain a large percentage of heavy elements. The outer regions have predominantly lighter elements.

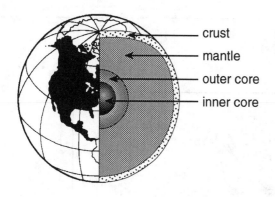

6. What does the earth's structure suggest about its history?

   A. It began as loosely packed material and was later sorted by gravity.

   B. It has continued to build up new layers on an original smaller planet.

   C. It began as a hollow ball that has been filled in by erosion from the surface.

   D. It originated from collisions of smaller planets of different densities.

Use the following information to answer questions 7–9.

Electromagnetic energy travels as waves.

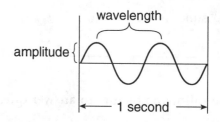

frequency = number of waves to pass a point per second

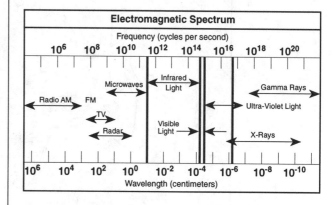

7. Which of the following properties is used to arrange the various types of waves shown?

   A. amplitude

   B. shape

   C. length

   D. origin

8. Which of the following types of electromagnetic radiation has a wavelength of 10^2 cm?

   A. TV signal

   B. infrared light

   C. visible light

   D. X-rays

9. As the wavelength increases, how does the frequency change?

   A. increases   C. remains constant

   B. decreases   D. no relationship

10. In a food pyramid, producers are able to use the sun's energy to make food. Which of the pictured organisms is a producer?

A.
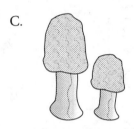

B.

C.

D.

11. In a food chain, energy is transferred from the sun through a series of organisms. Which set of organisms below is in the proper order for a food chain?

A. mountain lion, rabbit, berries, fox
B. fox, rabbit, berries, mountain lion
C. berries, rabbit, fox, mountain lion
D. berries, mountain lion, rabbit, fox

12. In an ecosystem, what is the function of decomposers?

A. to control the producer population
B. to release carbon for other organisms
C. to capture energy from the sun
D. to balance predator/prey populations

13. What is one reason that the United States regulates the cutting of trees for lumber?

A. Forests provide homes for wildlife.
B. The supply of tree seeds is limited.
C. Logging releases pollutants that cause acid rain.
D. Synthetic lumber substitutes are readily available.

14. What is the primary drawback to using nuclear power to produce electricity?

A. It is too expensive.
B. It is too inefficient.
C. Fuel supplies are limited.
D. It produces hazardous wastes.

15. Which of the following is considered a renewable source of energy?
    A. oil
    B. alcohol
    C. coal
    D. natural gas

Use the following diagram to answer questions 16 and 17.

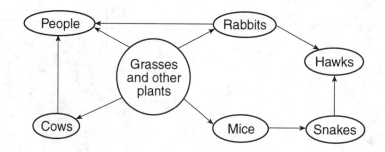

16. An increase in the mice population would most directly affect which of these organisms' population?
    A. cows
    B. hawks
    C. rabbits
    D. snakes

17. The loss of which organism would prevent energy from entering the food web?
    A. cows
    B. people
    C. plants
    D. snakes

18. Eurasian watermilfoil was introduced into the northeastern United States in the 1940s. This plant has spread to 30 other states, often crowding out native species. What is the most likely reason that it could do this?
    A. It was not part of existing local food chains.
    B. Humans do not consume it for food.
    C. Water plants spread faster than land plants.
    D. Foreign plants generally are hardier than native ones.

UNIT THREE

Extending Scientific Knowledge

The Ohio State Department of Education expects you to demonstrate the ability to perform 20 basic science tasks. Unit 3 reviews the following topics:

- Apply concepts of the earth's rotation, tilt, and revolution to an understanding of time and season. (Outcome 6)

- Apply the use of simple machines to practical situations. (Outcome 8)

- Apply the concept of force and mass to predict the motion of objects. (Outcome 9)

- Apply the concepts of energy transformations in electrical and mechanical systems. (Outcome 10)

- Explain biological diversity in terms of the transmission of genetic characteristics. (Outcome 15)

At the beginning of the last unit, science data were compared to rumpled laundry. Processing that data was compared to straightening out that laundry. Now think about why a person would do the laundry in the first place. It's because the clothes and other items will be used for something—for wearing, in the case of clothes. If something useless gets dirty, you probably don't bother to wash it.

Similarly, scientists have a better chance of getting funded to do their work if the results of their work promise to be useful for something. Inventions, predictions, and explanations all can be extensions of science research.

This unit features some extensions of science knowledge.

covery Module 7: Life Science

Act Like a Scientist

One of the real-life questions scientists have studied over the years is how human characteristics vary from person to person. Some differences, such as eye color, are clearly inherited. That information is carried in the chromosomes of each of your cells.

Units of information on those chromosomes are called genes. Sometimes a characteristic can have a range of differences. In such cases, more than one gene most likely influences that characteristic. This is the case with the measurement that you will take in the next activity.

Directions: Obtain the hand spans of at least 10 classmates. The more hand spans you measure, the more likely you are to obtain the expected results. Measure in mm as shown and record your results in the table on the next page.

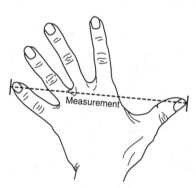

Measuring Hand Span

KEY WORDS   inherit   chromosome   gene

Person	Hand span	Person	Hand span

Make a bar graph showing the number of people with each hand span. The data should be grouped so that each bar represents the number of people within a 10 mm range (e.g., 120–129 mm).

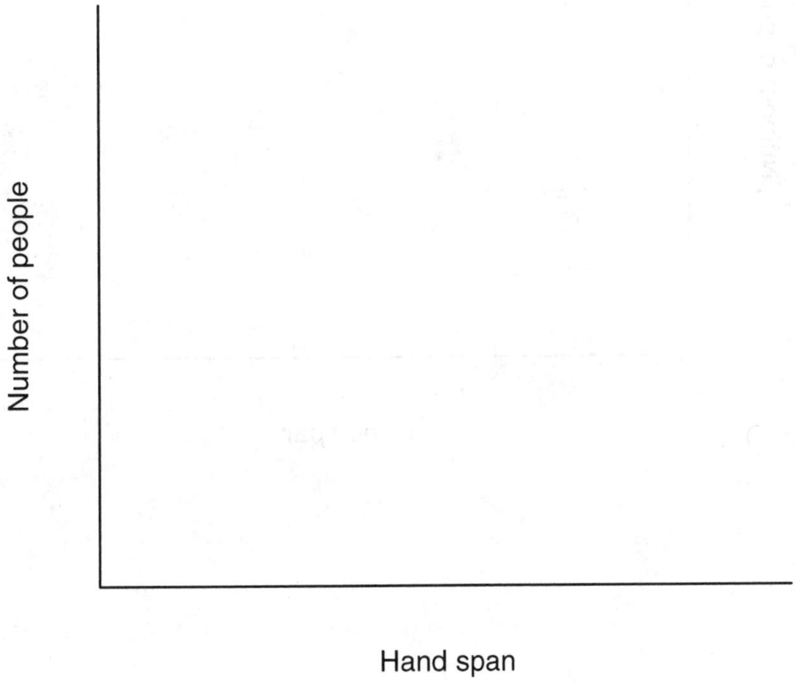

Number of people

Hand span

Fill in the table showing the number of people with each hand span. The data should be grouped in a 10 mm range (e.g., 120-129 mm).

Span Range										
Number of People										

Complete this bar graph. Each bar should represent the number of people in each cell on the bottom row of your table.

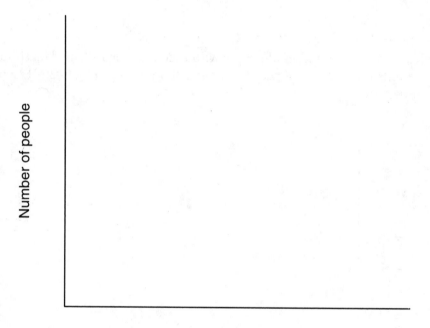

Hand span

Think Like a Scientist

1. Often, the data "clump" so that there are two peaks in the graph. What could be one explanation for this?

    _____

    _____

    _____

2. Why is there a wide range of data?

    _____

    _____

    _____

3. What other human data might be expected to form a broad range of results?

    _____

    _____

    _____

Test Like a Scientist

The study of genetics is useful in agriculture, as well as in human and veterinary medicine.

Use the following genetic information to answer questions 1–4.

- Traits for organisms are determined by pairs of gene forms called alleles.

- The pairs are formed by random pairings of one allele from each parent.

- A dominant trait will be expressed *if either one or both* of its alleles is present.

- A recessive trait will be expressed *only if both* of its alleles are present.

1. Of what use is the above information in the field of medicine?
   A. to help prevent infectious diseases
   B. to determine the likelihood of genetic disorders
   C. to help develop more effective birth control methods
   D. to treat people who have genetic disorders

   Reasoning: State your reason or reasons for selecting the answer. (Use a form of the terms "genes" and "inherit" in your reasoning.)

   _____

   _____

   _____

   _____

Use the following genetic information, in addition to the genetic "rules" on the previous page, to answer questions 2–4.

- For guinea pigs, black fur is dominant, white is recessive.

In several guinea pig litters from the same set of parents, the following occurred:

Coat Color	Total Number of Offspring
black	12
white	8

2. What conclusion can be drawn from these results?
   A. Both parents had an allele for a white coat.
   B. Only one of the parents had a white coat.
   C. Only one of the parents had a black coat.
   D. Both parents had an allele for a black coat.

   Reasoning: State your reason or reasons for selecting the answer. (Use a form of the words "recessive" and "dominant" in your reasoning.)

   _____

   _____

   _____

   _____

3. If two of the offspring with white fur were to have offspring of their own, what would be their chances of having offspring with black fur?
   A. 100%
   B. 75%
   C. 50%
   D. 0%

   Reasoning: State your reason or reasons for selecting the answer. (Keep in mind your answer to question 2.)

   _____

   _____

   _____

   _____

Use the following information, in addition to the information on pages 86 and 87, to answer question 4.

A Punnett square is a model that is often used to determine the likelihood of offspring having a particular trait. Dominant alleles are represented by upper case letters and recessive ones by lower case letters. The parents' alleles are written on the outside top and left of the square. The possible pairings in the offspring are then shown inside the square.

For example:

- In pea plants, green (G) seed color is dominant over yellow (g) seed color.

- If two parent plants each with an allele for both colors are bred, the Punnett square may be written:

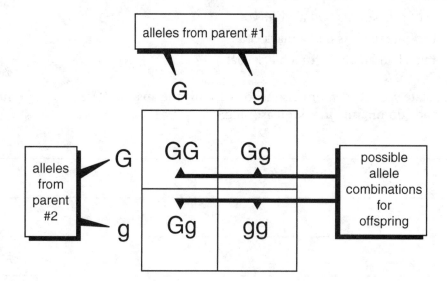

KEY WORDS   Punnett square

4. If B represents the allele for brown eyes, and b represents the allele for blue eyes, which of the following Punnett squares is the appropriate model for the offspring of two blue-eyed parents?

A.

	b	b
b	bb	bb
b	bb	bb

C.

	B	B
B	BB	BB
b	Bb	Bb

B.

	B	B
B	BB	BB
B	BB	BB

D.

	B	b
B	BB	BB
b	Bb	bb

Reasoning: State your reason or reasons for selecting the answer. (Show the possible allele combinations with the resulting eye color as part of your explanation.)

_____

_____

_____

_____

Evolution is an explanation for the changes in organisms over many generations.

Use the following pictures of bird feet to answer questions 5 and 6.

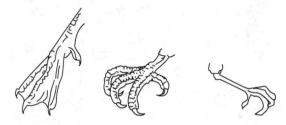

5. What is the best explanation for the variety of birds' feet shown?
    A. They are feet of the same type of bird at different life stages.
    B. They are feet of birds that evolved from different phyla.
    C. They have evolved from past successful mutations.
    D. They represent stages in the evolution of webbed feet.

    Reasoning: State your reason or reasons for selecting the answer. (Explain how organisms can change between generations.)

    _____

    _____

    _____

    _____

6. When were the foot characteristics determined?
    A. during the bird's adult life   C. while the embryo was in the egg
    B. while the bird was a nestling   D. when the egg was fertilized

    Reasoning: State your reason or reasons for selecting the answer. (Explain how genetic characteristics are transmitted to an offspring.)

    _____

    _____

    _____

    _____

  evolution   mutation

Discovery Module 8: Earth Science

Act Like a Scientist

Directions: Imagine that your head is the earth and that the head of a classmate is the sun. Ohio is located on your forehead and the equator is at the tip of your nose. Stand several feet from the "sun." Spend a few moments using your imagination to *feel* the light and heat from the sun that you are facing. The more you use your imagination, the more effective this activity will be. Then follow the steps below.

1. Slowly spin in a circle, to represent the rotation of the earth. When you are facing the sun, it is daytime in Ohio. When you are facing away from the sun, it is night in Ohio, but daytime in places on the back of your head—Asia, for example. Notice that nothing happens to the sun at night, you are simply turned away from it.

2. Now walk around the sun. The earth would keep spinning—after all, days and nights keep occurring all year long—but to keep from getting dizzy, just walk normally. In making one revolution, you complete a year's journey.

3. Next, you'll demonstrate the season changes that would have occurred during your walk. Look at the sun and tilt your head upward, so that your chin gets direct light from the sun. Imagine that your forehead is now cooler than your chin. It is winter in Ohio, which, you'll remember, is on your forehead.

4. Go to the opposite side of the sun. Now tilt your head downward so that your forehead is getting the sun's direct light. It is summer in Ohio.

5. During fall and spring, you would be halfway between summer and winter. Go to each of those positions and look directly at the sun (your partner, not the real sun). Your nose gets the direct light (and heat), while your chin and forehead get equal, but less direct, rays. In fall and spring, the sun's light is more direct than in winter and less direct than in summer.

Think Like a Scientist

1. Summarize what happens in Ohio during one rotation (full spin) of the earth around its axis.

    _____

    _____

    _____

2. Summarize what happens in Ohio during one earth revolution around the sun.

    _____

    _____

    _____

3. How are the seasons related to the directness of the sun's rays?

    _____

    _____

    _____

Test Like a Scientist

The study of our solar system is useful in understanding the effects of the sun and moon upon the earth.

Use the following diagram to answer questions 1 and 2.

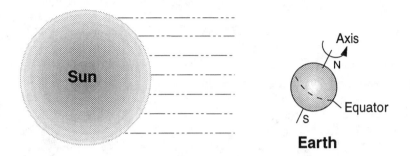

1. According to the diagram, what season is it in Ohio, which is roughly 40° north of the equator?

   A. summer   C. winter

   B. autumn   D. spring

   Reasoning: State your reason or reasons for selecting the answer. (In your explanation, use what you learned about the relationship between directness of the sun's rays and seasons in the "Think like a scientist" activity.)

   _____

   _____

   _____

   _____

2. Assume that Ohio is facing the sun in the diagram. When the earth rotates on its axis 180° (half a circle) from where it is now, what will occur in Ohio?

   A. summer   C. daytime

   B. autumn   D. night time

   Reasoning: State your reason or reasons for selecting the answer. (Include a diagram in your explanation.)

   _____

   _____

   _____

   _____

Use the following diagram to answer question 3.

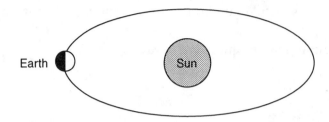

3. Which diagram shows Earth's position six months later?

A. 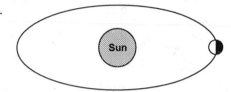   C.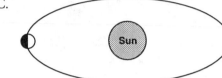

B. 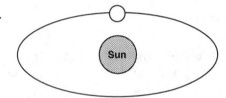   D.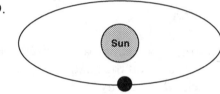

Reasoning: State your reason or reasons for selecting the answer. (First, describe the motion of the earth for a full year.)

_____

_____

_____

_____

Use the following picture to answer question 4.

4. This diagram could be used to explain which of the following?
   A. day and night
   B. phases of the moon
   C. summer and winter
   D. weather patterns

   Reasoning: State your reason or reasons for selecting the answer.
   (First, explain the diagram.)

   _____

   _____

   _____

   _____

5. If the moon were twice its present distance from the earth, what would be the most noticeable effect on Earth events?
   A. longer seasons
   B. lower tides
   C. shorter days
   D. colder weather

   Reasoning: State your reason or reasons for selecting the answer. (First, explain the moon's present effect on Earth events.)

   _____

   _____

   _____

   _____

Understanding the solar system requires specific information about its components.

Use the following information to answer question 6.

Planet Facts

	Mercury	Venus	Earth	Mars	Jupiter	Saturn	Uranus	Neptune	Pluto
Distance from the Sun (Millions of Miles)	36.0	67.1	92.9	141.5	483.4	886.7	1,782.7	2,794.3	3,666.1
Diameter (# of Miles)	3,031	7,521	7,926	4,221	88,734	74,566	31,566	30,199	1,864
Volume	0.06	0.86	1.00	0.15	1,323	752	64	54	0.01
Mean Orbital Speed (Miles per Second)	29.8	21.7	18.6	14.9	8.0	6.0	4.2	3.3	2.9
Revolution (Around the Sun)	88.0 days	224.7 days	365.26 days	687.0 days	11.86 years	29.46 years	84.01 years	164.8 years	247.7 years

6. Information in this table can be used to make which of the following comparisons between Earth and the other planets?

   A. strength of gravity

   B. length of days each season

   C. number of seasons per year

   D. time to complete one year

   Reasoning: State your reason or reasons for selecting the answer. (Explain how your answer choice affects the earth, and then extend it to the other planets.)

   _____

   _____

   _____

   _____

KEY WORDS   revolution   orbit

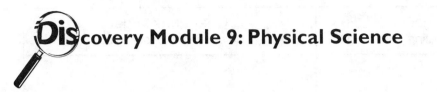

Discovery Module 9: Physical Science

Act Like a Scientist

Materials needed: Several sheets of paper (Notebook paper will work, but larger sheets are better.)
Coins: a quarter and a dime

1. Place the dime left of the middle of the paper and trace it. Write an "S" (for starting location) in the circle. Use the quarter as you would use a cue ball in billiards by sliding it into the dime. Be sure to release the quarter before the coins collide. Practice this several times until you can get both coins to remain on the paper after the collision.

   "Shoot" the dime with the quarter. Trace the coins in their resting positions. Repeat the procedure two more times, tracing the coins in their resting positions after each collision. Put numbers one, two, and three in the respective resting location circles after each trial.

   Draw the starting and resting positions for each trial in the left column of the table on the next page. Each box represents the sheet of paper on which you're doing this activity.

2. Turn your paper over or get a new sheet (as directed by your teacher.) Repeat the procedure three more times, but this time use the quarter as the target and the dime as the cue ball. Draw the results in the right column of the table.

	Dime as target (Draw the starting and resting positions.)	Quarter as target (Draw the starting and resting positions.)
TRIAL 1		
TRIAL 2		
TRIAL 3		

Think Like a Scientist

1. Compare the results between using a dime or a quarter as the target.

   _____

   _____

   _____

   _____

2. Explain the results of the collision.

   _____

   _____

   _____

   _____

   _____

   _____

3. What are some real-life situations demonstrated by this experiment?

   _____

   _____

   _____

   _____

Test Like a Scientist

An understanding of simple machines is useful in the field of engineering.

Use the following information to answer questions 1 and 2.

Levers can be used to increase the force used to move a resistance or to cause the resistance to move farther than the applied force. The product of the effort force (f_E) multiplied by its distance from the fulcrum (d_E) equals the product of the resistance force (f_R) multiplied by its distance from the fulcrum (d_R).

$$f_E d_E = f_R d_R$$

The three classes of levers are indicated in the diagram below.

Classes of Levers

First Class	Second Class	Third Class

Key   E = effort force   R = resistance force   F = fulcrum

1. Which class(es) of lever(s) can be used to increase the effort force?
   A. first
   B. third
   C. second and third
   D. first and second

   Reasoning: State your reason or reasons for selecting the answer. (Explain the relationship between distance and force.)

   _____

   _____

   _____

KEY WORDS   simple machine   lever   force   resistance force   fulcrum

2. What action will cause the resistance force to increase its speed relative to the speed of the effort force?

    A. Move the fulcrum toward the effort force.

    B. Move the fulcrum toward the resistance force.

    C. Move the fulcrum opposite the resistance force.

    D. Center the fulcrum between the effort and resistance forces.

    Reasoning: State your reason or reasons for selecting the answer. (Explain how time, distance, and speed are related.)

    _____

    _____

    _____

    _____

Use the following picture to answer question 3.

3. What change could the user of this wrench make to apply more force to the nut?

    A. Push the wrench from the bottom.

    B. Use the other end of the wrench.

    C. Grasp the wrench farther from the nut.

    D. Put a lubricant between the wrench and nut.

    Reasoning: State your reason or reasons for selecting the answer. (Use the distance/force relationship in your reasoning.)

    _____

    _____

    _____

    _____

Use the following diagram to answer question 4.

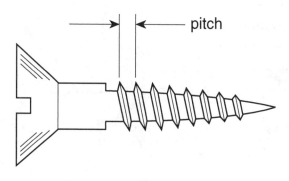

4. How will increasing the size of the screw's pitch affect the force required to turn the screw?
   A. decrease the force required
   B. increase the force required
   C. force will be the same
   D. cannot be predicted

   Reasoning: State your reason or reasons for selecting the answer. (Use the distance/force relationship in your reasoning.)

   _____

   _____

   _____

   _____

Use the following diagram to answer question 5.

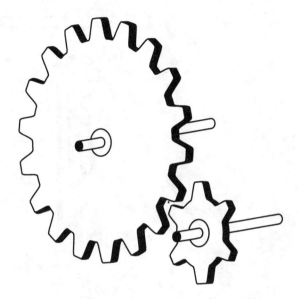

5. How does the amount of force required to turn the shaft holding the small gear compare with the amount of force transferred to the shaft holding the large gear?

A. less force to turn the small gear shaft

B. more force to turn the small gear shaft

C. equal force on both gear shafts

D. cannot be determined from diagram

Reasoning: State your reason or reasons for selecting the answer. (Use the distance/force relationship in your reasoning.)

_____

_____

_____

_____

Use the following diagram to answer question 6.

6. The mechanical advantage of the pulley system is 4. Which statement describes the system?
   A. The worker pulls the rope the same distance that the load moves.
   B. The worker pulls the rope less distance than the load moves.
   C. The worker's force is less than that required to lift the load directly.
   D. The worker's force is more than that required to lift the load directly.

   Reasoning: State your reason or reasons for selecting the answer. (Use the distance/force relationship developed earlier and explain the term "mechanical advantage.")

   _____

   _____

   _____

   _____

Knowledge of magnetism and electricity is important in construction, engineering, communications, and many other fields.

Use the following diagram to answer question 7.

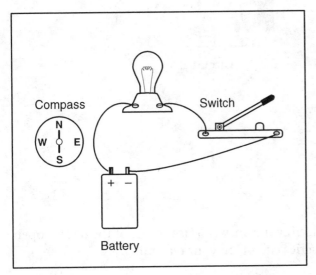
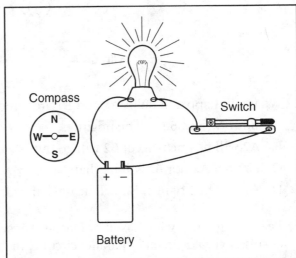

7. Which of the following can the compass needle detect?

A. light waves

B. ionization

C. radioactivity

D. electric current

Reasoning: State your reason or reasons for selecting the answer. (As part of your reasoning, explain how a compass works.)

_____

_____

_____

_____

Use the following diagram to answer question 8.

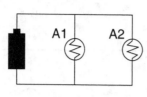

Circuit A   **Circuit B**

8. What will happen if bulbs A1 and B1 are removed?

  A. Both A2 and B2 will be brighter.

  B. A2 will be unchanged; B2 will go out.

  C. Neither A2 nor B2 will be changed.

  D. A2 will be brighter; B2 will be unchanged.

Reasoning: State your reason or reasons for selecting the answer. (Use forms of the terms "open circuit," "closed circuit," "parallel circuit," or "series circuit" in your reasoning.)

_____

_____

_____

_____

KEY WORDS   open circuit   closed circuit   parallel circuit   series circuit

The study of force and motion is important to aeronautics, highway design, mechanical engineering, and many other fields.

Use the following diagram to answer question 9.

9. What will happen to the suspended 50 g mass if the ball is swung at a slower rate?
   A. It will descend.
   B. It will swing in a circle.
   C. It will not change its position.
   D. It will be pulled up to the tube.

   Reasoning: State your reason or reasons for selecting the answer. (Use the term *centripetal force* in your explanation.)

   _____

   _____

   _____

   _____

KEY WORDS centripetal force

Use the following diagram to answer question 10.

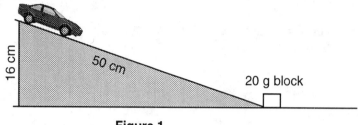

Figure 1

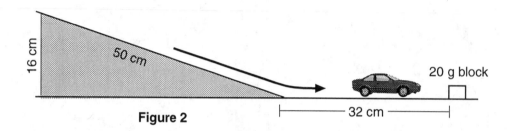

Figure 2

10. If the 20 g block is replaced with a 60 g block, what is the most likely distance that it would be pushed?

    A. 96 cm

    B. 48 cm

    C. 24 cm

    D. 12 cm

    Reasoning: State your reason or reasons for selecting the answer. (Restate how force and distance are related.)

    _____

    _____

    _____

    _____

Use the following diagram to answer question 11.

**Free-fall of a ball
as seen in strobe light**

11. Which graph indicates the ball's velocity during the fall?

A.

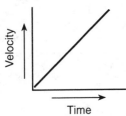

C.

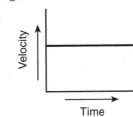

B.

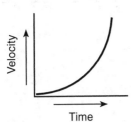

D.

Reasoning: State your reason or reasons for selecting the answer. (Define the word "velocity" in your reasoning.)

_____

_____

_____

KEY WORDS velocity

Use the following diagram to answer question 12.

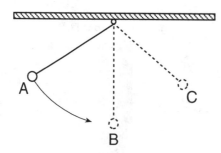

12. Which statement describes the pendulum bob's motion as it goes from B to C?
    A. constant velocity
    B. increasing velocity
    C. constant acceleration
    D. decreasing acceleration

    Reasoning: State your reason or reasons for selecting the answer. (Explain what forces are acting upon the pendulum bob.)

    _____

    _____

    _____

    _____

OHIO SCIENCE CONNECTIONS

Orville and Wilbur Wright were determined to fly. Working together in their bicycle shop in Dayton, Ohio, they designed and built an airplane that would change the world. Orville, who was born in Dayton, made the first ever successful flight in a self-propelled, heavier-than-air craft on December 17, 1903, near Kitty Hawk, at Kill Devil Hills, North Carolina.

The Wright brothers successfully combined thrust and lift to overcome weight and drag, forces that operate on all aircraft, as shown in the drawing below:

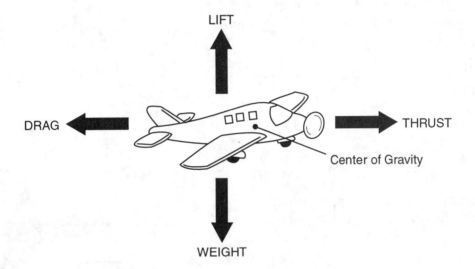

The aircraft wing is designed so that air flows over the upper surface at a higher velocity than it flows over the lower surface. The Bernoulli effect states that pressure drops as a fluid (air in this case) accelerates. Therefore lift is produced on the wing's top surface. But the wing also produces drag as it moves through the air. A wing cross section is shown below:

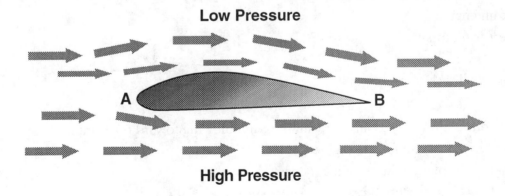

KEY WORDS   lift   drag   thrust   **Bernoulli effect**

Use the following diagrams to answer question 1.

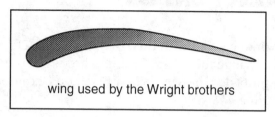

wing used by the Wright brothers

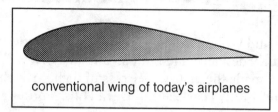

conventional wing of today's airplanes

1. The wing used by the Wright brothers would be unsuitable for modern aircraft because it
    produces a great amount of which force?
    A. lift
    B. drag
    C. thrust
    D. weight

Use the diagram at the right to answer question 2.

2. The streamlined shape of modern aircraft is
    designed to maximize the efficiency of which force?
    A. lift
    B. drag
    C. thrust
    D. weight

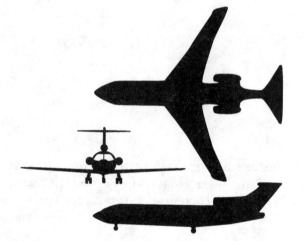

3. Which of the following inventions was key to the
    successful flight of heavier-than-air craft?
    A. steam engine
    B. electric motors
    C. gas-powered engine
    D. solid-fuel rocket engines

4. Why do pilots always try to take off with the wind blowing toward the front of their airplanes?
    A. to provide extra air for the engine
    B. to keep the plane from traveling too fast
    C. to allow them to stop in case of an emergency
    D. to increase the air speed over the wings

Get the BEST of the Test

Become an Editor of Science Tests

Try your hand at writing some test questions. Remember, becoming a better test maker will help you to be a better test taker.

Using the following diagram, write four possible test questions.

1. _____

   _____

   _____

2. _____

   _____

   _____

3. _____

   _____

   _____

4. _____

   _____

Use this pendulum data for question 5.

Length of String	Angle of Release	Period of Swing
40 cm	20°	1.27 sec.
60 cm	40°	1.55 sec.
80 cm	60°	1.80 sec.

Provide some possible answers for this question:

5. What appears to make the pendulum increase its period of swing?

A. _____

B. _____

C. _____

D. _____

Use this picture to write question 6.

6. _____

_____

A. _____

B. _____

C. _____

D. _____

Proficiency Practice

Directions: Read each question and answer choice carefully. Circle the letter of the correct answer. Be prepared to discuss your answers in class.

Use the following diagram of sun positions to answer questions 1 and 2.

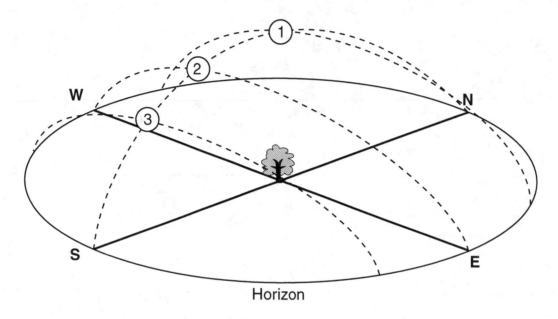

Horizon

1. Sun position 3 occurs during what season?
   A. winter
   B. spring
   C. summer
   D. fall

2. How much time passes while the sun moves from position 1 to position 2?
   A. 3 minutes
   B. 3 hours
   C. 3 days
   D. 3 months

Use the following diagram to answer question 3.

The vertical pole is in sunlight. The shadows are shown.

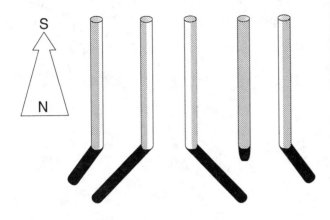

3. Which shadow properties would be most useful in placing the shadows in the correct time sequence?

    A. direction and length

    B. length and thickness

    C. darkness and direction

    D. thickness and darkness

Use the following diagram to answer question 4.

4. Compared to the large gear's shaft, how fast will the shaft attached to the small gear turn?

    A. slower

    B. faster

    C. equal

    D. can't be determined

Use the following diagram to answer question 5.

5. Which simple machine do the screw threads represent?

    A. pulley

    B. lever

    C. inclined plane

    D. wheel and axle

Use the following diagram to answer question 6.

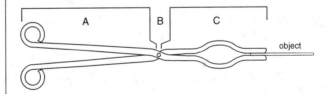

6. The amount of force squeezing an object held by the tongs is greater than the force squeezing on the handles. What factor determines this?

    A. size of section B

    B. curved shape of section C

    C. strength of the metal in section A

    D. relative lengths of sections A and C

Use the following diagram to answer question 7.

The tether ball is being swung as shown by the curved arrow.

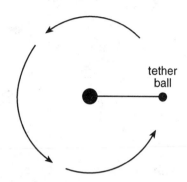

7. If the string breaks when the ball is at the point shown, which dashed line will be the ball's flight path?

A.
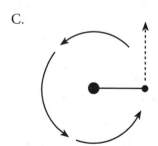

B.
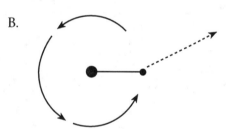

C.
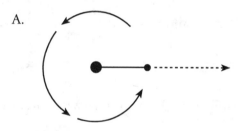

D.
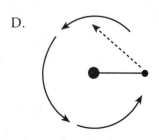

Use the following information to answer questions 8 and 9.

The relationship between the force, mass, and acceleration of an object (F = ma) is shown in the graph below:

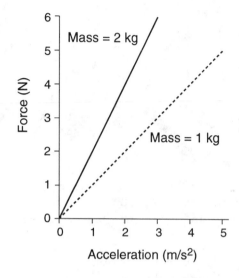

8. Based on the information in the graph, what acceleration would you predict at 4N of force if the mass is increased to 4 Kg?

A. less than 2 m/s^2

B. 2 m/s^2

C. 4 m/s^2

D. greater than 4 m/s^2

9. What conclusion can reasonably be drawn from this data?

A. Acceleration is independent of mass and force.

B. Mass, but not force, affects acceleration.

C. Force, but not mass, affects acceleration.

D. Acceleration is dependent upon both force and mass.

Use the following picture to answer question 10.

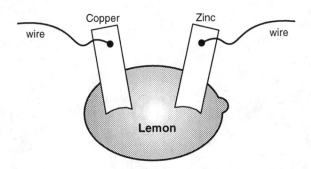

10. The pictured apparatus can be used as what device?

    A. battery

    B. timer

    C. pH meter

    D. thermometer

Use the following picture to answer question 11.

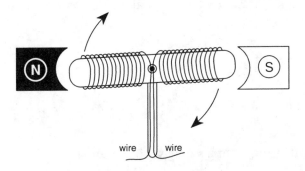

11. The pictured device is constructed to accomplish what energy conversion?

    A. heat to motion

    B. motion to heat

    C. motion to magnetism

    D. electricity to motion

Use the following diagram to answer question 12.

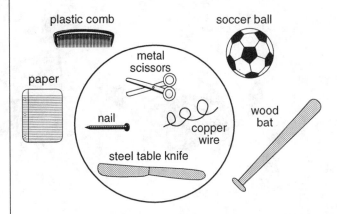

12. By what property are the groups of objects in the diagram most likely divided?

    A. type of simple machine

    B. number of moving parts

    C. ability to conduct electricity

    D. mass per square centimeter

Use the following pictures to answer question 13.

13. What accounts for the fact that these very different animals have all developed wings?
    A. Their ancestors figured out a way to get food more easily.
    B. Their wings were a successful adaptation to their environment.
    C. These animals have all evolved from the same winged ancestor.
    D. These animals are evolving toward being the same animal in the future.

14. The predictable physical changes that occur during the lifetime of an animal are due to which of the following?
    A. Different sets of genes are active at each stage.
    B. Natural selection of new characteristics occurs.
    C. Each gene can produce multiple characteristics.
    D. Each gene produces different characteristics at each stage.

15. Which statement helps to explain the variety of offspring from a single set of parents?
    A. The genetic code is not specific.
    B. Genes usually change after fertilization.
    C. Sex cell genes are unrelated to those in body cells.
    D. Forms of each gene combine randomly at fertilization.

UNIT FOUR

Science Then and Now

The Ohio State Department of Education expects you to demonstrate the ability to perform 20 basic science tasks. Unit 4 reviews the following topics:

- Identify and apply science safety procedures. (Outcome 3)

- Describe the ways scientific ideas have changed using historical contexts. (Outcome 17)

- Describe the relationship between technology and science. (Outcome 19)

Discovery Module 10: Science From the Past

On holidays and special occasions, many families get together to celebrate. These special days often provide an opportunity for a family reunion, a gathering of relatives from the oldest grandparents down to the youngest babies.

Science has a family too. The science family includes all the scientists who have made contributions to our present understanding of science. It also includes the present scientists, as well as all the students of science. Just as meeting with your relatives gives you a sense of who you are, meeting the science family can give you a sense of what science is and how it works.

This unit explores science history, science connections with technology, and science safety tips.

Act Like a Scientist

Before you meet with your relatives, you and members of your family probably talk about who those relatives are, and maybe about some of their special characteristics. "I wonder if Uncle Bob still has his worm farm," might be the kind of thing you'd say.

For this exercise, try to remember the names of three scientists, past or present. Write them on the lines provided. Then write what accomplishment is associated with each of them. You may need to use your science book, ask your science teacher, or search other references to help you with this.

1. Scientist: _____

   Accomplishment: _____

   _____

   _____

2. Scientist: _____

   Accomplishment: _____

   _____

   _____

3. Scientist: _____

   Accomplishment: _____

   _____

   _____

Think Like a Scientist

1. Why do you think people can generally recall the names of more entertainment and sports people than scientists?

_____

_____

_____

_____

2. In what ways might knowing some science history make science more interesting?

_____

_____

_____

_____

3. In what ways might knowing the history of a topic make it easier to understand that topic?

_____

_____

_____

_____

Test Like a Scientist

Studying the history of science provides a framework for understanding science today.

Use the following information to answer question 1.

In the late 1600s, Sir Isaac Newton published a work which described his well-known laws of motion. However, in the 1840s, astronomers pointed out that the motion of the planet Mercury was actually different than Newton's tables had predicted. It wasn't until a century later that Einstein's theory of relativity could explain this occurrence.

(By the way, the story of Newton discovering principles of gravity because an apple fell on his head is generally considered to be a myth.)

1. Which of the following statements is supported by the information above?
   A. Scientific ideas are seldom accurate.
   B. Scientific progress requires a lot of hard work.
   C. The laws of motion do not apply in space.
   D. Theories in science are modified by new evidence.

   Reasoning: State your reason or reasons for selecting the answer. (Pick out the supporting information in the passage.)

   _____

   _____

   _____

   _____

Use the following information to answer question 2.

Empedocles, a Greek philosopher-scientist, theorized that air, fire, water, and earth made up all matter. He also theorized that two forces were responsible for every event. The attractive force of *harmony* caused the "elements" to combine and the repelling force of *strife* separated them again. The same elements then entered into further events.

2. What modern scientific law is related to Empedocles' theory?
   A. laws of motion
   B. law of electric charge
   C. law of conservation of mass
   D. universal law of gravitation

   Reasoning: State your reason or reasons for selecting the answer. (Show how the notion of "recycling" elements is present in both Empedocles' theory and your answer choice.)

   _____

   _____

   _____

   _____

Use the following information to answer question 3.

The fossilized bones of Lystrosaurus, a hippopotamus relative of 200 million years ago, have been found in Antarctica. Other fossils of this animal were found in Africa. Such an animal could not survive in the climate of present Antarctica.

3. What theory is supported by the discovery of Lystrosaurus in both Africa and Antarctica?
   A. cell   C. the big bang
   B. evolution   D. plate tectonics

   Reasoning: State your reason or reasons for selecting the answer. (Explain how the climate of Antarctica could have been warm enough for Lystrosaurus at one time.)

   _____

   _____

   _____

Use the following information to answer question 4.

In the seventeenth and eighteenth centuries, scientists argued about whether or not cells could form "spontaneously" from nonliving materials. In 1749, a scientist named Needham performed several experiments in which he boiled a broth solution. The container was then sealed with a cork. After a while, living cells appeared in the broth. He concluded that cells could arise from nonliving materials.

Spallanzani, another scientist of the time, performed similar experiments. However, he boiled his broth for a longer time and sealed the container by melting its glass neck. Living cells never were generated in his solutions. His conclusion, supported by many experiments since then, was that cells form only from other cells.

4. What do these experiments illustrate about discoveries in science?
    A. They lead to advancements for humanity.
    B. They must be confirmed by other researchers.
    C. Not all discoveries are important to society.
    D. They were not very reliable in the early days.

    Reasoning: State your reason or reasons for selecting the answer. (What is the main idea of this passage?)

    _____

    _____

    _____

    _____

Scientific discoveries often lead to new technology.

Use the following information to answer question 5.

In 1752, Benjamin Franklin demonstrated that lightning is a form of electricity. This discovery led to a greater understanding of both lightning and electricity.

5. Which of the following inventions was a direct result of this finding?
    A. weather radar
    B. electric lights
    C. lightning rods
    D. welding machines

Reasoning: State your reason or reasons for selecting the answer. (Explain the connections between the invention and an electric current generated in nature.)

_____

_____

_____

_____

Use the following information to answer question 6.

In the late 1800s, it was discovered that certain wavelengths of electromagnetic radiation could pass through solid opaque material. At the time, this information was seen by scientists to be useful in defining the structure and mechanism of the atom. This information was also used to develop an important medical technology.

6. What modern medical technology developed from this discovery?
    A. x-rays
    B. fiber-optic scopes
    C. contact lenses
    D. laser surgery

Reasoning: State your reason or reasons for selecting the answer. (Explain how your answer choice uses the properties described in the passage.)

_____

_____

_____

Use the following information to answer question 7.

Genetic engineering can involve the artificial transfer of molecules containing genetic information between individuals of the same or different species.

7. Basic research in what general fields of science would most likely contribute directly to this technology?
   A. geology and biology
   B. biology and chemistry
   C. chemistry and physics
   D. physics and astronomy

Reasoning: State your reason or reasons for selecting the answer. (Explain the connection between each field and genetic engineering.)

_____

_____

_____

Use the following information to answer question 8.

Asbestos was once widely used as insulation because of its resistance to fire, heat, and corrosion. It is now being replaced because medical researchers have linked it to certain types of cancer.

8. This change shows an interdependence between what two fields?
   A. science and technology
   B. science and geography
   C. technology and geology
   D. medicine and meteorology

Reasoning: State your reason or reasons for selecting the answer. (First, define each of the individual terms.)

_____

_____

_____

Discovery Module 11: General Safety Procedures

In this module, you will have a chance to increase your knowledge of safety procedures and demonstrate that you understand how to apply them correctly. The following procedures are designed to increase your safety in commonly encountered school laboratory conditions.

Protective Wear

1. Wear safety goggles when you are working with chemicals, burners, or any substance that might get into your eyes. Your teacher may advise you of other situations in which you should wear goggles.

2. Wear a lab apron or coat when working with chemicals or heated substances.

3. If you have long hair, tie it back when working with laboratory equipment.

4. When experimenting, avoid wearing excessively loose clothing or hanging jewelry (such as dangling earrings or long necklaces).

General Rules

5. Read all directions thoroughly before starting a laboratory procedure. Ask your teacher for help if you do not understand the directions.

6. Perform only authorized activities.

7. Do not eat or drink anything while in the laboratory.

8. Wash your hands before leaving the laboratory.

Accidents

9. Immediately report all accidents to your teacher.

10. Learn what to do in case of accidents with specific materials. (For example, never use water to extinguish an electrical fire.)

11. Know how and where to report fires. Know the location of the fire extinguisher, fire blanket, phone, emergency phone numbers, and fire alarm.

Electricity

12. Inspect all electrical cords for damage prior to use.

13. Keep cords and electrical equipment away from water.

14. Never make direct contact with a live power source.

Heat

15.   Be aware that some substances that are harmless when cold are dangerous when heated.

16.   Remember that hot glassware may not look hot.

17.   Heat liquids only in open containers.

18.   While heating containers, always point the open end away from yourself and classmates.

Chemicals

19.   Never touch, taste, or smell unknown chemicals.

20.   Do not return unused chemicals to their original container. Dispose of chemicals only in the manner outlined by your teacher.

21.   When pouring acids and bases, hold the containers over the sink.

22.   Pour acids into water, never water into acids.

After an Experiment

23.   Clean up your work space and return all equipment to its proper storage area.

Act Like a Scientist

Make a map-like diagram of your science classroom. Note the location of the following, if present:

- fire extinguisher
- fire blanket
- safety goggles
- first aid kit
- safety shower

- eyewash
- telephone with emergency numbers posted
- fire evacuation route directions
- special trash container for broken glass
- lab aprons

Think Like a Scientist

1. Describe how to use the fire extinguisher in your room. (If you are not familiar with the proper procedure, ask your teacher to help.)

_____

_____

2. What kind of fires should it be used for?

_____

_____

_____

3. Where should the spray be directed?

_____

_____

_____

4. What should be done if someone's clothes catch fire? (Again, ask your teacher to help if you are not familiar with the proper procedure.)

_____

_____

_____

5. Which, if any, of the equipment listed in the "Act Like a Scientist" section is missing in your science classroom? What types of activities, if any, should be avoided due to the missing safety equipment?

_____

_____

_____

Test Like a Scientist

1. Which of the following statements does NOT describe proper procedure when dealing with chemicals?

   A. Never touch, taste, or smell unknown chemicals.

   B. Always read the labels on chemical containers.

   C. Wear safety goggles when working with chemicals.

   D. Carefully return unused chemicals to their original containers.

   Reasoning: State your reason or reasons for selecting the answer. (Think about both present and future hazards.)

   _____

   _____

   _____

   _____

2. An experiment requires a 10% solution of hydrochloric acid. Which of the following procedures should be used to prepare the solution?

   A. Add water to the concentrated acid without stirring.

   B. Add the concentrated acid to the water while stirring.

   C. Add the concentrated acid to the water without stirring.

   D. Add water to the concentrated acid while stirring.

   Reasoning: State your reason or reasons for selecting the answer. (Consider the heat produced by the combination of acid and water.)

   _____

   _____

   _____

3. After notifying your teacher, what is the best procedure to follow if you break a piece of glassware?

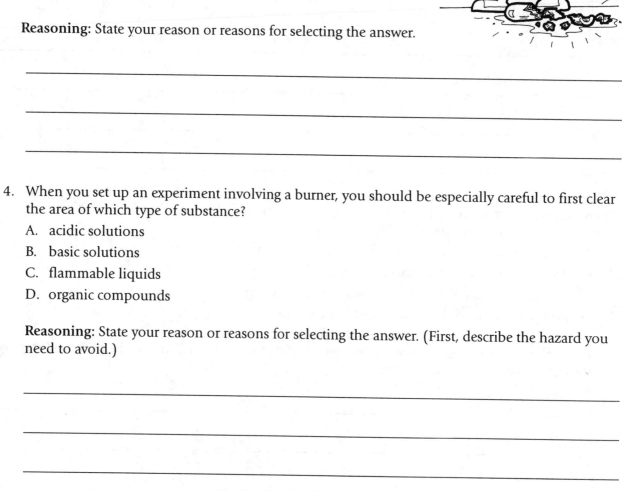

   A. Sweep up the pieces and put them in a waste container for broken glass.

   B. Quickly pick up the pieces and throw them in the wastepaper basket.

   C. Pick up the big pieces, sweep up the little ones, and place them in a waste container for broken glass.

   D. Push the pieces aside, and continue to work until the teacher has time to clean up the broken pieces.

   Reasoning: State your reason or reasons for selecting the answer.

   _____

   _____

   _____

4. When you set up an experiment involving a burner, you should be especially careful to first clear the area of which type of substance?

   A. acidic solutions

   B. basic solutions

   C. flammable liquids

   D. organic compounds

   Reasoning: State your reason or reasons for selecting the answer. (First, describe the hazard you need to avoid.)

   _____

   _____

   _____

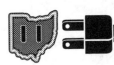 **OHIO SCIENCE CONNECTIONS**

Two of America's early space pioneers were born in Ohio. John Glenn, Jr., who was the first American to orbit the earth (February 20, 1962), was born in Cambridge. Neil Armstrong, who was the first person to set foot on the moon (July 20, 1969), was born in Wapakoneta.

1. Why do astronauts experience weightlessness when they orbit the earth?
   A. They are beyond the earth's gravitational field.
   B. The earth's gravity is balanced by that of the moon.
   C. Their centrifugal force neutralizes the earth's gravity.
   D. The spacecraft's speed outruns gravitational pull.

2. As of today, what is the farthest distance from Earth that astronauts have traveled?
   A. the distance to the moon
   B. the distance to Mars
   C. the altitude of the Space Shuttle's orbit
   D. the altitude of the Space Station Mir

3. Rocket engines used to launch space vehicles are different from jet engines used to propel aircraft because they
   A. make use of nuclear fuel.
   B. use internal combustion.
   C. are made to fire vertically.
   D. have a self-contained oxygen supply.

4. In the early days of space exploration, ground tracking stations around the earth relayed radio signals from orbiting craft to Houston's space command center. Why didn't the command center communicate directly with the astronauts?
   A. The distance to the spacecraft was too great for part of the orbit.
   B. Radio waves can travel only in straight lines through air or space.
   C. The spacecraft would have required too large an antenna.
   D. Transmitters on the spacecraft were not powerful enough.

Get the BEST of the Test

 Here's another opportunity to prepare yourself for taking a test by making one. You should first refresh your memory about the general safety procedures listed at the beginning of this unit.

1. Without looking back, list as many rules as you remember, plus any additional ones that you may have learned in science class. The headings may help you to recall rules for each category.

General Safety Procedures

Protective Wear: _____

_____

General Rules: _____

_____

Accidents: _____

_____

Electricity: _____

_____

Heat: _____

_____

Chemicals: _____

_____

After an Experiment: _____

_____

After you have filled in as many safety rules as you can remember, check the list at the beginning of the unit to fill in any that you missed.

Use the following picture to develop your own safety question:

2. What hazards can you spot in the picture?

_____

_____

Write a multiple-choice test item based on this picture.

3. _____

_____

A. _____

B. _____

C. _____

D. _____

Proficiency Practice

Directions: Read each question and answer choice carefully. Circle the letter of the correct answer. Be prepared to discuss your answers in class.

Use the following diagram to answer question 1.

In the diagram below, a scientist is inserting a glass tube into a rubber stopper.

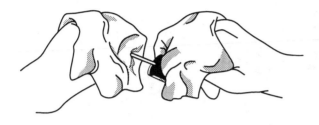

1. Why is this scientist using pieces of cloth to hold the apparatus?

   A. to prevent injury in case the glass tube breaks

   B. to avoid contaminating the stopper and glass tube

   C. to be able to apply greater force in inserting the glass tube

   D. to prevent the material on the lab ware from getting on hands

Use the following procedure to answer question 2.

An experiment includes the following steps in its directions:

   1. Put 50 mL of 10% hydrochloric acid in a beaker.

   2. Use a medicine dropper to add the acid to . . .

2. Which of the following pieces of equipment is the most important to use in this experiment?

   A.

   B.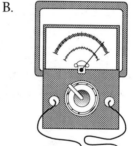

   C.

   D.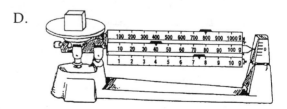

Use the following diagram to answer question 3.

3. Why is this scientist pouring the liquid onto the glass rod?

A. to dissipate any static electricity that may have built up

B. to cool the liquid before it reaches the beaker

C. to moisten the glass rod for later use in stirring

D. to guide the liquid into the beaker without spilling

Use the following information to answer question 4.

In the early 1900s, a scientist named Walter Sutton observed sperm and egg cells through a microscope. He noticed that each sex cell carried only half the number of chromosomes as the body cells of the organisms that produced them.

4. Based on the information above, which conclusion did Sutton most likely make?

A. Egg cells cannot fertilize other egg cells.

B. Genetic information doubles each generation.

C. Sperm and egg cells cannot become body cells.

D. Characteristics are transmitted from each parent by chromosomes.

Use the following information to answer question 5.

The Greeks in the time of Pythagoras believed that all of existence was governed by the laws of musical harmony. Later, Johannes Kepler tried to use the laws of music to explain the motions of the planets. While that attempt failed, it did lead Kepler to a successful mathematical framework that is now called *Kepler's Laws of Planetary Motion*.

5. Which statement follows from this information?

A. Music and science are unrelated.

B. Science knowledge builds on previous ideas.

C. Musical harmony cannot be explained by science.

D. Understanding science helps to understand music.

Use the following information to answer question 6.

While the planets visible to the naked eye have been observed for thousands of years, Uranus wasn't discovered until 1781, Neptune until 1846, and Pluto until 1930.

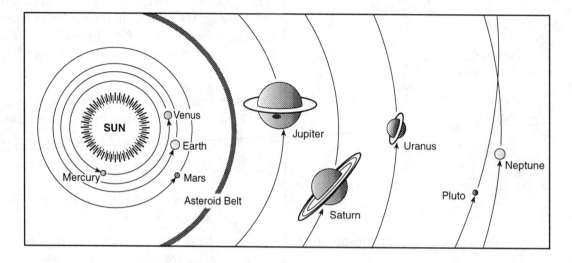

6. Which statement is best supported by this information?
   A. Current information about the solar system may change.
   B. Because information changes often, scientists cannot use it.
   C. Nothing new was discovered about the solar system after 1930.
   D. New moons will be discovered around the planets in our solar system.

---

7. While technology is developed using science principles, scientists also discover new uses for technology. Which statement is the best evidence for this?
   A. Rockets can be used in space as well as on earth.
   B. The automobile is used in nearly every country of the world.
   C. The telephone can be used to send many different messages.
   D. Lasers are used for surgery as well as analytical chemistry.

8. Alexander Fleming noticed that a certain mold was disrupting the growth of bacteria he was studying. What was developed as a result of this scientist's observation?
   A. a vaccine
   B. a vitamin
   C. an antibiotic
   D. a pesticide

Use the following diagram to answer question 9.

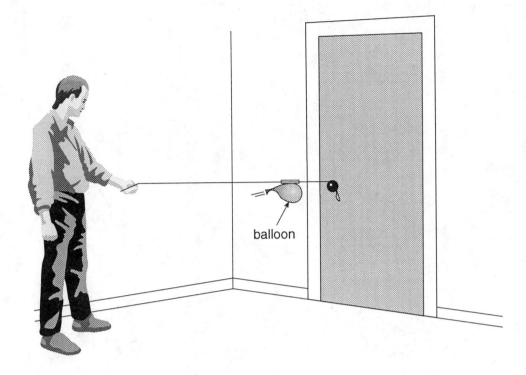

balloon

9. The science principle being investigated is related to what technology?

   A. helicopters
   B. rocket engines
   C. hot air balloons
   D. flight simulators

APPENDIX A

Student Proficiency Record

Directions: The record sheet on the following page will help you keep track of your progress toward mastering the state science outcomes. Record your scores by filling in the bubble for each question you have answered correctly.

After completing each test, count the number of questions you answered correctly. Write the total in the box at the bottom of the appropriate column. Once you have completed all five tests, count the total number of correct answers for each outcome. Write that number in the last box of that outcome's row.

Next, add your total scores together for all five tests. Write that number in the bottom, right-hand box. This will tell you your grand total score for all five tests.

Use your individual outcome scores and your grand total score to help you decide how to study. For example, you may decide to focus your efforts on a particular outcome or outcomes or choose to do a general review of all outcomes. Your teacher can best help you design a study program that meets your individual needs.

Ohio Science Outcomes	Proficiency Practice Questions				Diagnostic Test Questions	Total Score by Outcome
	Unit 1	Unit 2	Unit 3	Unit 4		
1. Devise a classification system for a set of objects or a group of organisms.	①②③				①②③	☐ /6
2. Distinguish between observation and inference given a representation of a scientific situation.	④⑤⑥				④⑤⑥	☐ /6
3. Identify and apply science safety procedures.				①②③	㊾㊿⑤④	☐ /6
4. Demonstrate an understanding of the use of measuring devices and report data in appropriate units.	⑦⑧⑨				⑦⑧⑨	☐ /6
5. Describe the results of earth-changing processes.		①②③			⑲⑳㉑	☐ /6
6. Apply concepts of the earth's rotation, tilt, and revolution to an understanding of time and season.			①②③		㊲㊳㊴	☐ /6
7. Describe interactions of matter and energy throughout the lithosphere, hydrosphere, and atmosphere.		④⑤⑥			㉒㉓㉔	☐ /6
8. Apply the use of simple machines to practical situations.			④⑤⑥		㊵㊶㊷	☐ /6
9. Apply the concept of force and mass to predict the motion of objects.			⑦⑧⑨		㊸㊹㊺	☐ /6
10. Apply the concepts of energy transformations in electrical and mechanical systems.			⑩⑪⑫		㊻㊼㊽	☐ /6
11. Apply concepts of sound and light waves to everyday situations.		⑦⑧⑨			㉕㉖㉗	☐ /6
12. Describe chemical and/or physical interactions of matter.	⑩⑪⑫				⑩⑪⑫	☐ /6
13. Trace the flow of energy and/or inter-relationships of organisms in an ecosystem.		⑩⑪⑫			㉘㉙㉚	☐ /6
14. Compare and contrast the characteristics of plants and animals.	⑬⑭⑮				⑬⑭⑮	☐ /6
15. Explain biological diversity in terms of the transmission of genetic characteristics.			⑬⑭⑮		㊾㊿⑤①	☐ /6
16. Describe how organisms accomplish basic life functions at various levels of organization and structure.	⑯⑰⑱				⑯⑰⑱	☐ /6
17. Describe the ways scientific ideas have changed using historical contexts.				④⑤⑥	⑤⑤⑤⑥⑤⑦	☐ /6
18. Compare renewable and nonrenewable resources and strategies for managing them.		⑬⑭⑮			㉛㉜㉝	☐ /6
19. Describe the relationship between technology and science.				⑦⑧⑨	⑤⑧⑤⑨⑥⓪	☐ /6
20. Describe how a given environmental change affects an ecosystem.		⑯⑰⑱			㉞㉟㊱	☐ /6
Test Totals	☐ /18	☐ /18	☐ /15	☐ /9	☐ /60	☐ /120

APPENDIX B

Glossary

acceleration	change in velocity over time
allele	one of the forms of a gene for a trait
amplitude	the height of a wave; its maximum distance from the position of rest; describes loudness of a sound wave
angle of incidence	the angle a light ray forms with a surface that it strikes
angle of reflection	the angle a light ray forms with a surface from which it reflects
atrium	a chamber of the heart that receives blood from the body and pumps it into the ventricles
Bernoulli effect	as fluids increase in speed, they exert less pressure
bilateral symmetry	having two identical sides when divided by a central line
boiling point	the temperature at which a substance undergoes a phase change from liquid to gas
capacity	a measure of how much of a substance a container holds; volume
carbon cycle	the continuous movement of carbon through the environment and organisms
carnivore	an animal that kills and eats other animals
cell	the smallest unit of an organism that can carry out life functions
cell wall	the rigid structure surrounding a plant cell; provides support to the plant

centripetal force	the force that causes an object to move in a circle
characteristic	a feature that helps distinguish an organism, object, or phenomenon
chemical change	the production of matter with new chemical properties
chromosome	a strand of DNA and protein that carries the code for an organism's inherited characteristics
circuit	a continuous conducting path from one terminal of a battery or power supply to the other
closed circuit	an uninterrupted circuit
compound	a pure substance that is created by chemically combining two or more elements; can be chemically broken down
condensation	a change in state from vapor to liquid
conservation	wise use of the earth's resources
consumer	an organism that cannot produce its own food; part of a food chain
contour map	a map that shows surface features by connecting lines at the same elevations
convergent boundary	a meeting of two tectonic plates that are pressing together
decomposer	an organism that makes nutrients available to an ecosystem by breaking down dead plants and animals
deposition	to lay down or leave behind particles that have been eroded elsewhere
divergent boundary	a meeting of two tectonic plates that are moving apart
dominant	an allele whose trait is expressed in either heterozygous or homozygous situations
drag	the force used to disturb the air
effort force	the force applied to a machine
embryo	a fertilized egg during its early growth
erosion	the wearing away of earth materials
evaporation	a change in state from liquid to vapor

evolution	gradual change in organisms over time
fault	a rock fracture along which movement occurs
food chain	the sequence of organisms through which energy is transferred
food web	an interconnected group of food chains
force	a push or a pull; tends to cause objects to accelerate
freezing point	the temperature at which a substance undergoes a phase change from liquid to solid
frequency	the number of waves to pass a certain point per second; describes pitch of a sound wave
friction	a force between objects in contact that hinders the motion of the objects
fulcrum	a rigid object used as a pivot for a lever
galaxy	a huge grouping of stars, dust particles, and other matter that has collected together in space; Earth is in the Milky Way galaxy
gas	matter that has neither definite shape nor definite volume
gene	a section of DNA that directs the production of a protein, and therefore a trait
graduated cylinder	a container with markings that can be used to measure capacity
gram	the basic unit of mass in the metric system
herbivore	an organism that eats only plants
host	the organism upon whose body a parasite lives and feeds
hydrosphere	the water in and on the lithosphere
inference	information logically derived from observations
inherit	to receive genetic traits from parents
intrusion	a magma flow that cools and hardens into rock before reaching the earth's surface
lateral boundary	a meeting of two tectonic plates that are moving sideways with respect to each other
length	a measure of the extent of something from one point to another

lever	a simple machine consisting of a rigid rod that can turn about a fixed point
lift	the force opposing gravity for an object in a fluid
liquid	matter that has a definite volume, but not a definite shape
liter	the basic unit of capacity in the metric system
lithosphere	the solid outer layer of the earth
mass	a measure of how much material an object contains
mechanical advantage	a machine's resistance force divided by its effort force
mesosphere	the layer of the earth's atmosphere located above the stratosphere
meter	the basic unit of length in the metric system
mitosis	cell division in which the offspring cells have the same number of chromosomes as the parent cells
momentum	an object's mass multiplied by its velocity
mutation	a permanent change in genetic material
nonrenewable resource	natural materials that exist in a definite quantity and are not being replenished as fast as they are being used up
observation	gathering of information through the senses, sometimes mediated by instruments
omnivore	an organism that feeds on both plants and animals
open circuit	an interrupted circuit
orbit	the path a smaller object follows as it travels around an object of larger mass; e.g., the moon orbits the earth
parallel circuit	an arrangement that allows electric current to flow through more than one path, allowing continuous operation if one path is interrupted
parasite	an organism that attaches itself to another organism (the host) and feeds upon it
pentagonal symmetry	five identical parts extending from a central point or axis—a special form of radial symmetry
pH	a measure that is used to describe how acidic or basic a solution is

phase change	conversion of one state of matter to another
photosynthesis	a process carried out by plants in which they utilize the sun's energy to convert carbon dioxide and water into sugar and oxygen
physical change	a change in a physical, but not a chemical, property of a substance
pitch	1. the highness or lowness of a sound, determined by the sound's frequency; 2. the angle of incline of a plane surface
plate tectonics	the theory that the earth's crust is divided into independently moving plates
predator	an animal that gains nutrition by killing and eating another animal
prey	an animal that is killed and eaten by a predator
producer	an organism that can produce nutrients by a process such as photosynthesis
Punnett square	a graphic means of representing possible allele combinations in the offspring of a set of parents
radial symmetry	identical parts extending from a central point on an axis; like spokes on a wheel
recessive	an allele whose trait is expressed in only homozygous situations
renewable resource	natural materials that can be replenished at the same rate as they are being used up
resistance force	the force provided by a machine
respiration	a process that occurs in all living cells in which energy is released by combining oxygen and food molecules
revolution	one complete spin of an object about its axis; e.g., the earth makes one revolution in a 24-hour period
series circuit	an arrangement that allows electric current to flow through only one path, which causes disruption of its operation if the path is interrupted
simple machine	a device that changes the size or direction of forces
solid	matter that has both definite volume and definite shape
spectrum	light separated by wavelengths; e.g., a rainbow
speed	the distance traveled by an object divided by the time needed to travel that distance

stratosphere	the layer of gases between the troposphere and mesosphere
symbiotic partners	a mutually beneficial relationship in which organisms are dependent upon each other
symmetry	identical appearance of parts on both sides of an object that is centrally divided by a line, plane, or axis
thrust	the forward force on an airplane or rocket caused by combustion of the fuel
trait	see characteristic
troposphere	the layer of the earth's atmosphere that contains water vapor
velocity	the speed of an object combined with its direction
ventricle	a chamber of the heart that pumps blood out into the body; a human heart has two ventricles
volume	a property of an object that describes how much space it occupies
weathering	erosion of rock into particles that eventually form soil

APPENDIX C

Hints for Taking Multiple-Choice Tests

Introduction

There's no substitute for knowledge when you take a test. You'll get the best results if you know the material that's being tested. But even knowing the material may not be enough if you don't feel comfortable taking tests. That's where a little test-preparation can help you.

Most people don't know *everything* there is to know about a subject. But they often know *something* about it. Studying will help you gain new knowledge. Test-preparation will help you make better use of the knowledge you gain. Both are important.

Let's start by taking a look at how a multiple-choice test question is constructed.

Dissecting a Multiple-Choice Question

- Multiple-choice test **items** (problems) are made up of a **stem** (usually a question) and several **responses** (sometimes called **answer choices** or **foils**).

- Only one of the answer choices is the **key** (the best answer).

- The other answer choices are intended to look attractive to a person who doesn't know everything they should about the material. These attractive, but incorrect, answer choices are called **distractors** (because they distract some people from the correct answer).

In the following **item**, circle the **stem** once and the **responses** twice. Underline the **key**.

1. Giraffes belong to which of the following vertebrate classes?
   A. fish
   B. reptile
   C. bird
   D. mammal

Increasing the Probability of Success

By learning how to eliminate choices that you know are wrong, you'll increase your chances of choosing the correct answer and of raising your score on the test.

Imagine for a moment that you have just read a multiple-choice test item that has four answer choices. It looks something like this:

2. Kjfzklf jklas jrljawk l34jlk 3ujoi?
   A. jkfjkjeiosr
   B. jies
   C. omelrj
   D. 324u4i

Whoa! How are you going to answer that one? You haven't even got a clue what the question is, let alone what any of the answer choices mean.

There's only one way. You've got to guess. Hmmmm . . . If you guess, what are your odds of choosing the correct answer?

The odds aren't too great—only 1 in 4, or 25%. Not good enough to pass the test, if all the items are as impossible as this one.

ZAP® the Obvious Wrong Choices

Instead of blind guessing, you need to learn to "Zero-in-And-Pick"—ZAP—before you guess.

Look at the next example:

3. Which of the following types of animals is able to fly?
   A. *Chiroptera*
   B. *Felis tigris*
   C. *Perissodactyla*
   D. *Proboscidea*

Another tough one. Do you recognize any of the answer choices?

How about B? Even if you weren't totally sure, you might take a guess that *Felis tigris* is some kind of a cat. It happens to be the Bengal tiger, an animal that makes some pretty amazing leaps when chasing after its prey, but that has never been known for any other kinds of aerial abilities. You can ZAP B.

Okay, so you've ZAPPED one answer choice. Your odds have just gotten better. Now you have a 1-in-3 chance of choosing the correct answer. Increasing your odds on a single item may not seem like much of an improvement, but increasing your odds on the entire test may make the difference between passing and failing.

Now that you know how ZAPPING can increase your odds, let's zero in on using it for multiple-choice tests.

Getting the Best of a Multiple-Choice Test Item

 Read the stem carefully.

In a well-written test item, the stem will set a definite task. For example:

4. Rocks are classified by their method of formation. Which of the following categories contains rocks that are formed by volcanoes?
   A. igneous
   B. marble
   C. gypsum
   D. sedimentary

Analysis

What's the **task** in the item above? To determine which of the listed rock categories contains rocks that are formed by volcanoes.

The stem asks for a rock **category**. Think back to earth science class. The categories of rock formation are igneous, sedimentary, and metamorphic.

Neither marble nor gypsum is a rock category, so *ZAP* B and C. You've just narrowed the answer choices to two, thereby improving your odds from 1-in-4 to 1-in-2. What is the correct answer?

 Reread the stem until you understand the task.

You may need to reread it more than once, but don't spend all morning on the same stem. If you can't understand it after two or three readings, you're probably better off going on to the rest of the test. The light bulb in your head may start to glow after you turn the page. You can always go back to answer it.

Examine any accompanying text or graphics.

You may be tempted to try to answer a question without taking time to study the text or graphics that accompany it. The additional material provided is there for a reason. Study it and you may well get the correct answer. Skip it and you'd better hope it's your lucky day.

For example, you might see a question like this:

5. During what approximate time span did the greatest increase in atmospheric sulfate occur?
   A. 850-1000
   B. 1200-1350
   C. 1450-1600
   D. 1800-1950

Pretty tough, isn't it? Now look at the information provided with the question.

Use the information below to answer question 5.

By sampling cores of ice in Greenland, scientists have been able to determine the average amount of atmospheric sulfate there during the past several hundred years. The graph summarizes the findings.

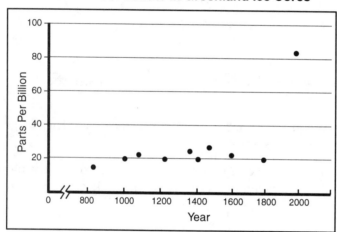

5. During what approximate time span did the greatest increase in atmospheric sulfate occur?
   A. 850-1000
   B. 1200-1350
   C. 1450-1600
   D. 1800-1950

Analysis

First, what's the task? To determine the time span in which the greatest increase of atmospheric sulfate occurred.

A quick look at the graph shows a dramatic rise from the data point at about 1800 to the next data point at about 1950, showing a sharp increase in the amount of sulfate in Greenland ice cores. However, the graph doesn't say anything about *atmospheric* sulfate. You had to read the paragraph in order to know that scientists are using the ice core data to determine levels of atmospheric sulfate.

Without examining the additional information, you would have no more than a 1-in-4 chance of guessing correctly. If you paid close attention to the paragraph and the graph, you should have a 4-in-4 chance! What's the answer?

Read all responses before making a final choice.

This will help you *ZAP* partially correct responses. For example:

6. Which of the following is an *incorrectly* ordered series of spectrum colors?
    A. blue, indigo, violet
    B. red, orange, yellow
    C. orange, green, pink
    D. green, violet, blue

Analysis

The task is to identify an *incorrectly* ordered series of spectrum colors. You might be tempted to pick C, because it does not represent three proper spectrum colors. But only D contains actual spectrum colors in the *incorrect* order.

Narrow your choices by ZAPPING the obvious wrong responses.

When two opposite responses appear, quickly *ZAP* the one that is least likely to be correct. This will give you fewer choices to consider. For example:

7. Compared to skin with a low density of nerve endings, skin with a high density of nerve endings will have which of the following?
    A. increased sensitivity to touch
    B. decreased sensitivity to touch
    C. broader range of stimuli felt
    D. narrower range of stimuli felt

Analysis

What's the task? To determine how skin with a high density of nerve endings compares to skin with a low density of nerve endings.

Two pairs of opposite answer choices, what a break! In each pair, *ZAP* the opposite that makes the least sense.

Then make a choice from the two remaining responses.

Which do you choose?

Be alert for clues in the stems of other items.

For example:

8. The colors of the spectrum, in order, are: red, orange, yellow, green, blue, indigo, and violet. Which one has the longest wavelength?
   A. blue
   B. indigo
   C. red
   D. yellow

Analysis

Hey, this could help with the example item for number 4 on the previous page. They've listed the spectrum colors in order.

By the way, if you're given a list in a question about shortest, tallest, or lightest, etc., the ending "est" tells you that the answer will be at one end of the list. Which one is it in the question above?

 Once you determine that a response is incorrect, do not consider it again.

If you are allowed to write in the test booklet, cross off the letter of any responses that you have already eliminated. If you can't decide between the ones remaining and have to come back to it, you won't waste time considering the same issues over again. (Of course, if you're using a scan sheet to record your answers, you'll need to be careful not to make any extra marks.)

 If no response can be ZAPPED, do not guess immediately.

Mark an X next to the item and go on. Sometimes the correct answer will occur to you while you are thinking of something else. Return to it later.

 DO NOT LEAVE ANY BLANKS.

There is no penalty for incorrect answers on this test. But don't just blindly guess until after you have followed all the tips above.